Dependent Arising In Context

To Ted, Miri and Dave
who have supported me in my work
in more ways than I can count

and Professor Richard Gombrich
who edits with generosity and good humor, and
who has given the Buddhist community so much

Dependent Arising In Context

the Buddha's core lesson
in the context of his times, and ours

Linda S. Blanchard

N
Nārada Publications via the CreateSpace
Publishing Platform

Published by Nārada Publications. Printed using the CreateSpace Independent Publishing Platform

Artwork by Annie Blanchard © 2012

The paper "Burning Yourself" was first published in the May 2012 edition of the Journal for the Oxford Centre for Buddhist Studies, Richard Gombrich, editor.

The series of posts "A Secular Understanding of Dependent Origination" saw first light on the website for the Secular Buddhist Association, secularbuddhism.org, released from May-June 2012.

The lone post "Words of Dependent Arising: Sankhara" appears on the author's website: justalittledust.com/blog

Library of Congress Cataloging-in-Publication Data:

Blanchard, Linda S.

Dependent Arising In Context: the Buddha's core lesson in the context of his time and ours / Linda S Blanchard

ISBN 10: 1481259547 (paperback)

ISBN 13: 978-1481259545 (paperback)

1. The Buddha, ca. 485-405 BCE. 2. Dependent origination I. Title.

Contents

Overview & Introduction

Overview Of This Book

This book is suitable for anyone interested in Buddhism who has studied and understood the basics ("The Four Noble Truths" and "The Eightfold Path") and who has at least begun to dig a little more deeply (into "The Three Marks of Existence" – dukkha/suffering, not-self, impermanence) and who is interested in going a bit further. If you've had a look at the teaching called "dependent arising" and not been satisfied with the explanations you've read, this book is definitely worth your time.

Anyone who has made even a brief study of dependent arising will likely realize that there are many different and sometimes conflicting explanations of what it is and what it means. Some think it is quite simple; they may be missing the complexity built into it. Those who have studied it most tend to admit that it seems a hopeless tangle. Part of the problem may be that this is the deepest and most detailed of the lessons the Buddha taught, and it is actually multi-layered, which has added to the confusion in the past. More important are the problems caused by the loss of the context of his times which have been obscure to, or ignored by Buddhists for millennia.

This book offers a completely new theory about the structure of this critical teaching that makes the lesson much easier to understand, and along the way straightens out many of those old tangles.

Because those approaching this topic will be coming from a wide variety of backgrounds and levels of understanding, you, the reader, will be best able to decide whether to read the somewhat scholarly paper that is presented first, before the series of articles on its application, or giving the series on the Secular Understanding a reading first, with the assurance that the reasons for this interpretation will be found in the paper. Perhaps flip a coin and try whichever luck brings, and if it doesn't make sense on first reading, persist and reread after both have been read; or go ahead and reverse what fortune brought (it's amazing how often we think we can't decide, then that coin flip comes out 'wrong' and we suddenly discover we had an opinion after all).

Once the two primary chapters have been understood, those who want to go deeper may want to read the detail on the one word, *sankhara*.

A note, on my choice to use unaccented Pali in about half of the book: I am aware that this may drive scholars crazy, and if so, I'm sorry for that. For the most part this book is intended to reach those who have a deepening interest in Buddhism and its practice, but who aren't academics. My preference is to make the text easy to read; I am not much concerned with Pali pronunciation, either. If the terms become familiar over time, they will no doubt be pronounced a variety of ways, in various local accents. It's the ideas that matter, more than the words themselves. I trust that the scholars will be able to figure out which Pali words are intended.

CITATION NOTES:

Within the text of this book, suttas are referenced by the abbreviated name of the volumes they are found in, for example "MN 117" stands for the 117th sutta in the book called "Majjhima Nikāya". "DN" stands for Dīgha Nikāya, "SN" for Saṃyutta Nikāya, "AN" for Aṅguttara Nikāya, "Dhp" for the Dhammapada, "Sn" for the Sutta Nipāta, "It" for Ituvatakka, and "Ud" for Udāna. Specific locations of quotations within the texts are referred to by the Pali Text Society ("pts") page numbers, as follows:

- pts = Pali Text Society
- a letter designation for the volume:
  - M (Majjhima Nikāya)
  - D (Dīgha Nikāya)
  - S (Saṃyutta Nikāya)
  - A (Aṅguttara Nikāya)
  - Sn (Sutta Nipāta)
  - I (Ituvatakka)
  - U (Udāna)
- a roman numeral for the book within the volume
- an Arabic numeral for the PTS page number in that book

Introduction

This book presents, for the first time in one place, two original works on dependent arising, the core lesson of the Buddha's complex system of insights that can lead us to a better life. In addition, there is one extra chapter just on the subject of one critical word used in the definition of dependent arising.

The first section is a paper called, "Burning Yourself" that was published in the Journal of the Oxford Centre For Buddhist Studies in May 2012. The original audience for this paper was assumed to know quite a bit more than the average person does about the content of the oldest works we have that are attributed to the Buddha (the Pali canon)—as well as having some familiarity with what was going on in the society the Buddha grew up and came to fame in. Even so, the paper was written to be understandable to a wider audience. It uses mostly non-technical language, and defines terms and the use of foreign words when they are first introduced. The paper describes what can be seen to be a previously unrecognized framework underlying dependent arising. This was a structure that elegantly expressed the point of the Buddha's "dharma" (his system of teachings, the "truth" that he wanted us to see) in a way that was clearly a pointed statement about the doctrines he was arguing against, at the same time describing a better way to see the world, with enough precision to remain useful to us 2,500 or so years later.

The second section of this book reprints a series of blog posts that may still be freely available on the website of the Secular Buddhist Association[1]. They were published in May through June 2012, written for an audience interested in Buddhism and Buddhist practices who might be looking for a better approach to understanding this deep teaching than the ones that traditional forms of Buddhism have handed on—because what our teachers have been telling us about dependent aris-

[1] At `http://secularbuddhism.org/`

ing has seemed, to many of us, to be less than satisfying (a point I will return to below, when I quote Ñāṇavīra). The blog posts were intended to describe what the Buddha was saying with his teachings on dependent arising in ways that a modern practitioner could understand and apply to their lives. That this teaching is suitable for a secular approach to Buddhism—one with no reliance on beliefs about phenomena not in clear evidence—comes from the nature of the teaching itself (it is a secular teaching) rather than through any effort on my part to remove elements of faith from it. This is evident when the original context and shape of the teaching is understood. Whereas the traditional interpretations of dependent arising see it as being a discussion of how our actions generate karma that results in rebirth (and rebirth doesn't fit into secular practice), dependent arising—with its original context restored—isn't about rebirth, though it does make extensive use of the language of rebirth to make its points. This is where the confusion comes in: the language has gotten confused with the point.

The third chapter of the book is drawn from my own blog, and focuses just on the word "*sankhara*" that was used by the Buddha in the definition of his central lesson. This word has always been a challenge for translators, myself among them. Only after publishing both the paper and the series of blog posts did I come to see what *sankhara* actually is—this definition is drawn from its place in the creation myth that underlies dependent arising—and this post was my attempt to try out the new definition in every significant context I could find in the suttas. I think the way that the new definition works so well is supporting evidence for the hypothesis in the paper.

I am not the first person (and will not be the last) to have begun to suspect, when reading the old texts, that the Buddha was not being literal when he talked about rebirth—either his past births, or the births of others. The idea that he was speaking metaphorically did not originate with me, but has been pointed out by many before me. The problem with this interpretation has always been with understanding why he would have sounded so literal when actually speaking metaphorically—why wouldn't it have been made as clear as could be that he was speaking metaphorically?—and how could he have been framing his teachings, using the language of rebirth, yet be understood in his time to mean anything else? It seems improbable on the surface, which is why many traditional Buddhist see the "metaphorical rebirth" view as a much-distorted reinterpretation of the Buddha's teaching. Yet all that it reinterprets, really, is the traditional understanding—it is an effort at restoring what was there in the original texts, but has gone unnoticed for millennia. The structure of dependent arising, in the context of his times, makes sense of how it could be that he was speaking metaphorically yet the texts don't explicitly say so, and we can also see why the traditions might have come to fail to understand this one small but very significant aspect of the teaching.

The series of blog posts were written for an audience who hadn't necessarily read the paper "Burning Yourself" (since it was then only available for a subscription to the Journal, and so was not widely read by Buddhists outside academia, and few enough in) but since the conclusions in the posts were drawn from the structure examined in the paper, reading the paper and getting at least an initial grasp of what it is about is very helpful in understanding how to apply the insights in dependent arising to our lives. Reading the paper first—even if not every word of it is clear on first pass—will make understanding the reasoning behind the blog entries easier. The reason this book exists at all is to put the two together in one place so that they will be readily available to anyone with an interest. As a way of giving back to the Journal that first published the paper, a portion of the profits from the book (if any) will be spent on subscriptions to the Journal.[2]

This book is not in any way intended to convince a follower of any of the ancient lineages of Buddhism to give up their present understanding of dependent arising in favor of this one. I follow Ñāṇavīra Thera's approach to presenting a new theory here:

> This Note will take for granted, first, that the reader is acquainted with this traditional interpretation, and secondly, that he is dissatisfied with it. It is not therefore proposed to enter into a detailed discussion of this interpretation, but

[2] The first one goes to me so that I can, hopefully, participate in any responses that get published in the letter column, but if this book sells more than a handful of copies, generating enough profit to go a little further, I will underwrite others' subscriptions with a portion of the proceeds so that others who are interested in reading and writing to or for the Journal, but are also on a tight budget, can also join in. If that happens, there will be information on my blog at `http://justalittledust.com/blog/` on how to apply.

> rather to indicate briefly that dissatisfaction with it is not unjustified, and then to outline what may perhaps be found to be a more satisfactory approach.[3]

With those lines, Ñāṇavīra spoke directly to me, all the way from beyond his grave, back to the living mind that addressed his dharma-siblings present-and-future with unabashed but unconceited straight talk about what he found when studying the suttas (sermons and stories) in the old texts, and putting them into practice (since both study and application are necessary to deep understanding of what the Buddha taught). It was Ñāṇavīra who first gave me insight into what the texts were actually trying to convey, insights that sometimes seemed to be outside of the traditional interpretations[4], though he did continue to believe that literal rebirth was part of the Buddha's view of the world. I was so thankful to find someone who had been willing to see for himself what the texts said, and to speak up when he found something different, but I was almost equally grateful to simply find that there was someone well-versed in the Pali canon who agreed that there was something wrong with the traditional interpretations, because that was where I had started from in my attempts to understand dependent arising.

I had been reading about Buddhism since the mid-80s, when my solitary and stubborn 32-year-old self married for the first time and found sharing a house and a life threw me so far off balance that I lost my generally happy nature and became someone even I would not have wanted to live with. Buddhism seemed to have some answers, and meditation did help, so I stuck with it though I confess to having been aware, at the time, that I didn't quite understand the teachings, and this was true for most of the decade that followed. When I finally did come to get what the Buddha was saying about how we create our own problems through our relationship to impermanence and "the self and the world", I dug in deeply, committing myself to both the practice and the sort of study that would deepen my understanding. Next I decided (inevitably, if you know my history) to write about what

---

[3] Ñāṇavīra Thera, in the introductory paragraphs to "A Note on Paṭiccasamuppāda" which can be found in his *Notes on Dhamma* (1963) or *Clearing the Path* (1987), both of which are available through Path Press, or free for reading online at `nanavira.org`. For those with the patience to pencil in translations of Pali as they go along (or those fluent in Pali), I highly recommend studying the Notes.

[4] This is my thanks to him and to everyone in the past, present, or future, who uses a similar approach in being willing to take a fresh look at the texts, to test understanding of them in life, and to be willing to stand up and state what they see, and continue to stand against the powerful tide of the status quo.

I had come to find so useful, to share the graceful simplicity at the heart of it with others while, simultaneously, giving myself a deeper education by studying the oldest texts and making sure that I could describe them well, and that I could find evidence in the texts that my understanding was accurate. This had the natural effect of showing me where my understanding was weak, and making me work to improve it. I began working on a book that would explain each element of the Buddha's teaching in a way that just about anyone could understand, and this project was moving along just fine until I started researching dependent arising.

It quickly became clear to me that not only did I not understand it, but no one whose writing I read on the subject understood it well enough to explain it to me in any convincing way, either. It was through my continued efforts to get a grip on what clearly was the single most important—the absolutely central—teaching in the Buddha's system, that I discovered Ñāṇavīra Thera's writings, which started me on a project of even deeper reading in the suttas. The more I read, the more it became clear that it was critical to understand dependent arising because so many other teachings referred to it, and then the more mind-boggling it became that traditional explanations weren't well-supported by what I was reading in the ancient texts.

Sticking to the texts didn't seem as though it was going to provide a solution—no doubt others had been trying this in monasteries for centuries—and if the answer was in the texts, it wasn't obvious. Along the way I encountered books by Richard Gombrich[5], who pointed out possible references to the Upanisads in Buddhist texts, which led me to step outside the texts to try to unlock the meaning through setting the teachings in the context of the times. I was wondering how many of the terms that remained unclear might be specific references to competing schools and teacher's systems in the Buddha's day, outside references that Buddhist monk-scholars through the years would not have spent much time studying, but that are getting thorough scrutiny under the study of Sanskrit scholars in universities all over the world nowadays. Reading about the Vedas and studying the styles of speaking in the Upanisads—which are thought to have been composed shortly before and some during the time of the Buddha—I began to find links between the two competing systems, Vedic and Buddhist.

Then, in an issue of the Pali Text Society's Journal, I discovered an article written in 2000 by a professor of Sanskrit, Joanna Jurewicz[6],

5 *How Buddhism Began* and *What The Buddha Thought*

6 "Playing With Fire" in Vol. XXVI of the Journal of the Pali Text Society.

which focused on the terms used to describe the classic twelve links of dependent arising, tying them to Vedic texts, and in particular to the Prajapati myth of "The First Man" also known as "The Lord of Creatures" since it was out of him that the whole world was created. I knew that myth was key not only to the world-view of people of the time, but to self-view, and to rituals centered on "the self" (*atta* in Pali, *atman* in Sanskrit). Jurewicz' article turned out to be the key that unlocked the last door.

The final point that might be useful to consider, before reading the paper and the articles that follow it, is the question of how the texts we have could have come down to us with something so central to the whole of them remaining obscure, yet with enough of the original still retained so that we can still locate the structure underneath. How could the context have been lost?

The only answers lie mostly in the realm of conjecture, though the conjecture relies on principals that are generally well-known and accepted, like, for instance, the way people transmit stories and texts in general, and "sacred texts" specifically.

What follows, then, is what I see as having happened, none of which I would attempt to "prove" but I simply leave for your own consideration.

In the times in which the Buddha lived, no one in the area was writing down sacred texts. There may have been writing during his time or shortly thereafter—it appears as though "keeping the books" for accounting purposes may have been the first use of writing in the area—but in his time and the centuries shortly thereafter, the suttas were passed on orally, with each work memorized by monks assigned them, and then those sermons were carried out into the wider world by the monks who walked them into villages and towns and distant cities to spread the Buddha's dharma far and wide.

Now when it comes to "oral transmission of stories and ideas" we are all familiar with the way what we start with can sometimes bear little resemblance to what arrives at the end of a line. Some of us have, at an early age, played "whisper the secret" around a circle and been surprised to find how distorted the message gets when passed on in this way. There is plenty of evidence, too, for creative stories and myths that are passed on from one generation to the next being changed from one story-teller to the next just as a matter of style, and even some substance being changed to suit the cultures and times a story passes through.

But in the Buddha's day—and over many centuries before and after him—there was a long and treasured history of passing sacred texts on from one person to the next very faithfully. The Vedas and the Upanisads, and the intervening texts, were passed on this way. Memorization was a highly prized skill, and texts tended to have incorporated into them many devices to help ensure that nothing was lost. This is one reason why so many lists in the Buddhist texts are numbered—there are "Four Noble Truths" and an "Eightfold Path"—you know when you've left one out, if the famous name tells how many there should be. There are other tricks, like little lists being ordered by the length of the words—and there are whole chunks of texts (called "pericopes"[7])—that represent key elements that are repeated pretty much word-for-word from one sutta to the next, to cut down on what needs to be memorized anew, and to make it easy to double-check against someone else who has memorized the same piece within a different sermon.

There is evidence that the main force of the efforts of monastics who passed on these texts was in honoring their 'sacred' nature and so changing them as little as possible[8] This means that the elements of oral story-telling in which style was important—the tendency of each speaker to imprint a story with their own characteristic flair—would be eliminated in favor of preserving both the style and the substance of the original speaker. Still, we are talking about texts that were passed on by copying one from the next, and that went through changes in the language conveying the message, both changes of grammatical fashions within one language, and changes from one language to another. The main body of the oldest texts we have are in "Pali" which was a language specifically designed—and seemingly created long after his death—to carry his message; it is a simplification and streamlining of the original languages which are thought to have been in the Brahmi family.

Another factor to consider is that most of these texts may have originated in the Buddha's own lifetime, with fresh sermons being memorized by monks in the area at the time, and then carried outward to

[7] Pronounced "pur-RIK-uh-pees".

[8] For example, in a post on my personal blog, I have examined two versions of one sutta that were well-separated in time—the version we have as passed on to us in the Pali canon, and a very old copy discovered in the area around Afghanistan, written on birch bark—and the essence of the story remains the same though the framing elements were a little different in each. (`http://justalittledust.com/blog/?p=768`).

distant communities (this was part of the entertainment and educational system of the day, having itinerant monks beg alms at the door and provide a sermon, along with, perhaps, news of people encountered along the way), but these sermons were not actually gathered up into what we call "the canon" until sometime after the Buddha's death. The volume of works for monastics (the Vinaya) tell of a "first council" in which the canon was first repeated and perhaps organized, but we also have tales of second and third councils, centuries afterward, and we can well imagine that over time, at some point, every effort would have been made to gather up every story, and every variant of each, as they had been passed down and sent outward over time.

Amongst these stories there are likely to have been some created "on the fly" by monks in distant lands who wove various pericopes from this sutta and that together into a new sermon that suited their needs in the moment—so we may have suttas that weren't created by the Buddha at all as such, but are made up of pieces of things he said elsewhere. And it could well be that some few of those put pericopes together in ways that end up having him imply things he might not have actually meant to convey—thus confusing things for us.

Along the same lines—and here we begin to get into how the structure of dependent arising might have been lost—we need to consider the job of the editors of the canon, who were collecting the stories from hither and yon and gathering them into official volumes, neatly ordered and numbered so that nothing would be lost. When they collected all these versions of the Buddha's talks, they would inevitably find a few that didn't seem to fit with the rest, that didn't make sense to their understanding of what the Buddha taught. They would see these as corruptions. Examining such texts, if they could see that the problem lay in just one portion, perhaps they would cut that out. Or if there was just one word, or there were a few, that said something that contradicted what they thought was meant, they might try to figure out how a copying error had introduced a mistake, and 'correct' that. If the whole lesson seemed wrong, they'd assume it was a fake, and not include it, so that it would be lost to us altogether.

All of which is fine, and a logical part of the editorial process, and it changes nothing as long as the understanding of the editor is perfectly aligned with what the Buddha taught in the first place. But what if editors of the text were part of a lineage that had misunderstood some part of the Buddha's message in some way? What effect would the process outlined above have on the texts? Wouldn't it tend to eliminate all evidence that there was ever any other way of looking at what the

Buddha was saying?[9] What if, somewhere along the way, the Buddha's disciples split into factions, with disagreements over what he meant by this or that? What if there were so many factions that no single one of them got everything the Buddha said precisely right? Buddhist history includes such factions—they were given a specific number in the high teens at one point early on—and while we don't have a great grasp of what each of them was about, it is clear that all but one of them will have had to get something wrong—only one could conceivably have everything perfectly right, and maybe not even one, if they divided over more than one issue (and on one split we have good detail on, it was several issues, which was probably typical).

The question might be: who won? Many of these lineages seem to have disappeared; some of them may have stayed around long enough to have some of their ideas blended back into the survivor's lines. The Theravada school of Buddhism—which brings us the Pali canon—will no doubt have evolved out of one of those original divisions. They are convinced that theirs is the one true account of the Buddha's teachings, and of course they could be right, but I think the evidence in the texts indicates that they didn't get everything right, because things got lost along the way. For example, Theravada has had no recognition of the language of the Prajapati myth being integrated into dependent arising, yet it will be quite clear to anyone with an open mind, and a bit of time to study the society of the day, that it is—so they certainly lost something, and it was an important something. Which means they don't have everything right, because they don't have an accurate understanding of everything in the texts.

When I think, objectively, about a large number of factions, each believing different things about what the Buddha taught, I ask myself not "Who won?" but "Why would the winner have won?" What do we know about how humans operate, that would give us insight into why one idea wins out over another? The newly minted idea of "meme theory" works well as a way of looking at the possibilities here[10], because it sees "ideas" as having qualities that make them more likely to be

---

[9] A living example of this sort of thinking, and this sort of process, can be found online in a thread on the wonderful forum Dhamma Wheel, in which the person who makes the original post presents a long thesis on why MN 117 is corrupt. If this person had been an editor of the canon, MN 117 would have been thrown out or modified. Fortunately there are many bright scholars of Buddhism on the forum, who are able to point out the holes in logic. `http://www.dhammawheel.com/viewtopic.php?f=13&t=14592`

[10] There isn't room in this book, much less in the introduction, to cover meme theory but there is plenty of good information on it on the internet, or you could read the book that started it all, Richard Dawkins' *Selfish Gene*.

passed on (just like genes do), and of having what can be perceived as "defense mechanisms" that keep them from being taken down by the competition (just like a virus does). Looked at that way, it would be easy to see how, in a society that became increasingly convinced that rebirth was the cosmic order, any time the Buddha talked about rebirth (regardless of what his deepest intention was) his words could be taken as a literal statement that he had knowledge of rebirth. Taken on just their surface, they certainly indicate that he did.

A rebirth-based doctrine would have had many advantages in his time: it would not have contradicted the status quo of the day too much (it would have been seen as simply an improvement instead of a revolution) and so would have had an easier time catching on; the dharma is much simpler to understand at entry-level as just being about rebirth, karma, and merit-making, than understanding not-self (*anatta*) which is actually the point. A system that allows for concern with our own future post-death[11] does say that something to do with us continues on, and we have many chances at doing better, which is a much more comforting message than "this may be your only chance—don't waste it!" At first glance, the idea of "not self" is not only *not* comforting, it is disconcerting—rebirth in any form is preferable to most people over not knowing, or the possibility that there is no continuation post-death. For these reasons, the meme of "the Buddha taught literal rebirth" has much greater viability than does his deepest teachings about letting go of certainty, and working only with what we can see for ourselves.

If one—or even several—of the factions in existence early on in the history of the transmission of the Buddha's dharma came to believe that he was teaching that rebirth is the cosmic order, that view would have a fair chance of becoming the winner. The view that he was not saying that there is rebirth would have been quite unpopular in the centuries following his death, when the idea of karma's effect on cyclic rebirth was gaining followers who would lead that doctrine on to what would become (what we know as) Hinduism. Having a teacher who says "I actually don't know what happens after death, and I don't care too much about it either" would be an unlikely winner in a contest against those who were certain about rebirth.

If there were competing views of what the Buddha meant when he talked about rebirth, then we know which view won. To the winner

[11] And no matter how many hocus-pocus tricks one plays with the concept of not-self to say that it isn't "us" who moves into the future, why else would we be concerned with the effects our acts in this life have on "us" in the next? Can't have it both ways; either we are concerned with self in the future or there is no self in the future so we are not.

goes the writing of history, and I find no reason to be surprised if there is little evidence surviving to show that there was ever anyone who believed otherwise. But you may have noticed I said, "little evidence", not "no evidence"—I'll explain this in a moment.

First, I want to point out that I am not suggesting that anyone ever came along and intentionally changed what they knew the Buddha to be saying to subvert his message and make it their own. This could have happened—there were certainly enough Brahmins in the flock to have had a few who were wolves put on sheepskin robes and consciously work to move Buddhism closer to their way of seeing the world. But the outcome we seem to have—of the slightly misunderstood teaching—doesn't require any kind of a conspiracy. All it requires is sincere monastics who believed they understood what was being said, who did their best to pass on what they understood, and for that message to be a strong enough meme to transmit itself and defend itself against all alternative understandings of the Buddha's teachings. The process of gathering and passing on the texts—correcting errors, and throwing out any "fakes" that clearly said the Buddha wasn't being literal—would take care of the rest.

If this hypothesis is correct (that there was an original teaching in which the Buddha was not talking about literal rebirth; that literal rebirth is a meme that took over without conscious effort to expunge the original teaching; that the effort to pass on the Buddha's message was a sincere attempt to pass it on correctly) then there could be—maybe even should be—some evidence of the older teaching visible through the dust of ages. And I believe there is.

There are texts in the suttas that indicate that the Buddha saw belief in rebirth as counterproductive; they survive because they can (with some effort) be interpreted as not saying that, but saying something else. In the parable of the arrow[12], we have the Buddha explaining that concern about the Cosmic Order does not lead to awakening; in many he denies that his teaching has anything to do with two polar-opposite view of eternalism[13] and annihilationism and says that, instead, he

[12] MN 63

[13] The eternalist view is given as being about cyclic rebirth, so the traditional take is that the Buddha is just denying that it is the self that is reborn, or that others are talking about "eternal" rebirth and he's talking about rebirth one can end. But the Vedic system was also suggesting there were ways to "escape the rounds" of rebirth (so they weren't really eternalists), and in his denials he does not say that his only objection is that what is defined as a self gets reborn; he has suggested we go look for anything **at all** that we can find that is "ours" (to do with us) that will move on to a future life, and asks us if we find it. In MN 1 he offers a very long list of ways people in his time perceived of (this or that) as "theirs"—detailing the many ways people

teaches dependent arising; and in one[14] he specifically points out that karmic systems and rebirth into "other worlds" are part of a view that tends to foster concern with the self, and he sets his own teaching apart as transcending those views. These are clues I have stumbled on without making any focused effort to find support for a 'view' of the Buddha not teaching literal rebirth; I was simply, actively trying to understand what is there. Often people who strongly believe the Buddha taught literal rebirth pointed such texts out to me, and a close reading of the Pali revealed that the texts could easily be read in more than one way, as long as they are approached with an open mind. To the various clues in the suttas, add the structure of dependent arising, and I believe there is a strong case for understanding the whole of the Buddha's teaching to have, originally, been secular.

If, over time, the words of the Buddha were preserved more-or-less accurately, with only a small number of deletions, insertions, remixes, and adjustments to language, how, then, would the understanding of what dependent arising meant be lost? There might be many factors that played into the effect.

The Buddha was constantly redefining terms common to his day—giving each his own specific twist (so that, for example, karma's "action" became "intention", which was his way of showing that it's why we do what we do that is critical)—and so the key terms of dependent arising could easily have come to be understood and defined as being different from their original meaning, and in fact seeming to make no reference at all to the originals. This may be true of "*sankhara*" which became completely disconnected from its origins, taking on a definition that was understood as "technical" with a specific (and obscure) Buddhist-only meaning. With its context lost, and only the obscure "technical" meaning of the word to go on, no change in a single sentence that the Buddha uttered about *sankhara* was needed to pull the meaning of what he was saying away from the original intent. Over time, the focus on the Buddha's unique spin on the word would ob-

conceived of some aspect that might move on to a future life, and he says we are mistaken in thinking it is true of any of them. I do want to make it clear that when he says that his teaching isn't about eternalism or annihilationism, he isn't saying either of those views is a misrepresentation of reality (he is not saying, "They are untrue and I know the way things actually work"), he is saying "It is wrong to hold such views when we have no evidence for them, and holding such views without clear evidence leads to trouble." If we pay attention to the texts, we find that in virtually every one he is not saying that he knows the actual answer of what happens after death—it is not because the view has been proven wrong that he says that it is wrong, it is because the view hasn't been proven at all, or because of the behavior it leads to.

14 MN 117

scure its origins even further, and the loss of the origins worked, in circular fashion, to make understanding the word even more difficult, until we come to our modern age, in which that one word gives translators a great deal of trouble (whereas restoring the context restores the sense—see the bonus chapter at the end of this book for detail).

Another factor might be that, at the outset, the structure was so well understood to be what it actually was—everyone will have understood the reference he was making (even if not everyone understood the point he was making with that reference)—that he never explicitly says what the words referred to. As I point out in "Burning Yourself", to take the time to explain context that was well known to everyone would be like stopping to explain the days of the week, belaboring the obvious. Since there was no reason to point out what the structure was, it apparently wasn't even discussed in his lifetime, and there would have been no need to talk about it for a generation or two afterward. Only when the social phenomenon he was practically parodying with his lesson had begun to fade into the background would his listeners need to be told what the structure was referring to, and by then those believing he was talking about literal rebirth would have had no interest in the origins of the structure, because they'd have had their own opinions about what his point was[15].

These might be a few among many factors, and there might be many clues that will help reveal the evolution in understanding of the dharma, and the timing of changes in perceptions about it. Scholars with more life left than I have, and greater access to ancient works that can be compared—the Gandharan scrolls, and Chinese agamas, for example—might be able to do a lot through examining and comparing texts. All I can offer here are possibilities, and the few texts I've come across in the short time I've been studying them. And a promise to keep on studying for as long as I can—and I will.

Scholars with such access, though, aren't the only ones who can contribute. I wonder how many more examples there are of texts that can easily be read two ways—the traditional way and in a way consistent with this understanding of dependent arising and the Buddha's teaching as secular—that would be discovered by other open-minded readers examining the texts. I hope this book will encourage those

[15] Words do change their meaning that fast, and we quickly lose any recollection that they ever meant something else. Our word 'silly' originally meant 'happy, blissful, lucky' eight hundred years back. It then morphed to mean 'spiritually blessed, pious, holy' and then it changed to 'innocent, harmless'. Next it came to mean 'deserving of pity, feeble', and finally, three hundred years after its origin, became 'foolish, simple', having gone through five sets of meanings in just those three centuries.

who are getting more involved in their practice to deepen their studies of these ancient discourses we are so fortunate to have access to. I invite you to have a look for yourself. And for those who love languages, start poking into the Pali (check the Resources section at the back of this book).

All that's left is for me to set you loose to read the book, and to thank everyone who has helped me with my research, and with comments on these works while they were in development. This especially includes Dave Bridges and Ian Challis, without whom I'd have given up long ago.

As always, anything useful you find in these pages will not have come from me, but has been brought about by causes, beginning with the amazing insight and elegant discourses of our original teacher from clan Gotama (aka "the Buddha"), followed by the valiant efforts of many who passed on the oldest texts, and more recently, the diligence of those who have studied these subjects before me and shared their understanding with others. Any failings belong to me and me alone.

Burning Yourself

Paṭicca Samuppāda *as a Description of the Arising of a False Sense of Self Modelled on Vedic Rituals*

Chapter 1: Burning Yourself

Paṭicca Samuppāda as a Description of the Arising of a False Sense of Self Modelled on Vedic Rituals

Purpose of this Paper

This paper offers a fresh interpretation of "dependent arising" (*paṭicca samuppāda*) as a description of how and why we humans create many of our own problems (experienced as *dukkha*) through a false sense of "self" (*attā*). That description was originally modelled on a worldview popular during the Buddha's lifetime, namely, the practice of rituals designed to create and perfect one's "self" (*attā*) in a way that would give the best results both in this life and after death.

This new view of the teaching offers a description that would have been quite clear to the people of the day. By seeing how obvious the setting would have been to the contemporary audience, we can better understand why the steps have seemed so obscure to us: the context, so clear at the time that it needed no further explanation, has been lost to us. Being both shorn of its context in real life, and devoid of detailed explanations of that context, has resulted in the loss of some of the finer points of the lesson.

In addition, the way the Buddha's culture used multileveled meanings has not been given enough weight, so that attempts to straighten the teaching into one linear description of events have run afoul of the multivariance of the message. I hope to show that explaining the context and structures brings what is being said into sharp focus, revealing an insight into human nature that is consistent with the rest of the Buddha's teaching, and is as valid and useful now as it was more than two millennia ago.

Supporting evidence for this theory will be provided primarily from *suttas* in the Pali canon, with some substantial help from certain modern texts that provide background information and current theories on the history of the culture in and around the Buddha's time. I will first present my overall theory, and then discuss the meaning of each of the classic twelve conditions and show, using evidence drawn from the *suttas*, how this new view makes sense of the data.

Conventions and Assumptions

No one knows with certainty whether most of the texts we find in the Sutta Piṭaka of the Pali canon were composed (or at least approved) by the Buddha himself, or were put together shortly after he died, or a long time after. Nor do we know whether they are somewhat modified from their original structures and wording, or greatly modified. In my reading of the *suttas*, I find, as many have before me, a consistent voice and personality. Whether that voice belonged to a real teacher or was created as part of a fictional story line has small impact: someone came up with this insight, and we might as well call him the Buddha. In the end it may make little difference when the teaching was put together or by whom, as long as the result is something we can understand and recognize as fitting well into the history of thought at that period. If the final structure turns out to have insights that are still useful to us in our time, all credit to the originator, whoever that may have been. For the sake of convenience, I will refer to the person who came up with both the insight and its structure as "the Buddha" and not concern myself about who or when, since that is not the point of this paper.

When attempting to understand a text, starting from the assumption that it is an indecipherable mashup of ideas, and maybe corrupt to boot, is logically unsound. It is best to begin by assuming the text is a coherent and well reasoned whole, unless research proves otherwise. My starting assumption, then, is that dependent arising has a uniform structure and a consistent message.

This does not mean that every piece of the Pali canon will necessarily fit into this understanding of what is being said. I acknowledge that there are likely to be corruptions introduced by later voices. Nonetheless, it seems safe to assume that if a large proportion of *suttas* dealing with *paṭicca samuppāda* fit this theory, it may be no less accurate, and perhaps more accurate, than some earlier interpretations.

For the most part I will try to confine the language used in this paper to ordinary English. I supply some Pali terms for reference, and the commonest among them I use in rotation with their English translations, just for the sake of variety; but there are a few terms that I will use in preference to their usual English counterparts because they make more sense when the reader is not left to draw on the established connotations of the terms commonly used in translation.

Foremost among these is *dukkha*, the full understanding of which should bring the awakening the Buddha hoped we could find through his words: the meaning of *dukkha* is precisely what the Buddha taught. In Pali *dukkha* has its opposite in *sukha*, often translated as "happiness"; so *dukkha* could be translated as "unhappiness", but is usually (inadequately) translated as "suffering". What it is, very roughly, is all that we experience through our own doing that takes us away from joy and especially from equanimity. Trying to give *dukkha* one English definition, or even many, confines it in unsuitable ways.

Another useful word is *dhamma*; its Sanskrit equivalent, *dharma*, has become widely used. The word was used to refer to various teacher's systems of helping others to see "what is" or "the way things work", and those are the primary senses of the word: as a truth, or a teaching about the truth, or a reality, that which "is". By default, most of the Buddha's uses of the word seem to indicate his own *dhamma*, the "truth of the way things are" that he describes.

Karma (*kamma* in Pali) has already entered into popular vocabulary, so to use its Sanskrit-derived popular form *karma* seems the simplest course.

The words *ātman* (*attā*) and *anatta* represent particular concepts. *Ātman* describes the Vedic understanding that there is an identifiable and lasting "self"; *anatta* is the Buddha's denial that any such thing can be found, a denial that points to what we mistakenly identify as *ātman*. Because these two words refer to ideas that have no exact equivalent in English, and are critical to an understanding of dependent arising, I will use the Pali more often than their longer definitions in English. Though in the *suttas anatta* is defined by what it is not—the Buddha seems at great pains to keep from giving it concreteness—in my own understanding, there is "something" there. What that "something" is, is "an ongoing process".

In the same way that we identify "the process by which things burn" as "fire" and treat "fire" as if it were a thing, the Vedic people identified *attā* as a thing, while the Buddha indicated that it was not a thing, and pointed out that it was like fire. Most people seem to have assumed that the self was a fixed and identifiable entity within each sentient being.

One term seems to have been a challenge for all translators: *saṅkhāra*. In its place as the second step of *paṭicca samuppāda* it is a key term. It has often been translated in recent times as "volitional formations" and one dictionary defines it as an "essential condition; a thing conditioned, mental coefficients".[16] It may be all those things, but it is above all the key to unlocking the meaning of dependent arising. I will therefore leave its definitions until later, and will frequently use the Pali form rather than translations, just as I leave *dukkha* untranslated.

Its Place in the Buddha's *Dhamma*

> "Now this has been said by the Blessed One: 'One who sees dependent origination sees the *dhamma*; one who sees the *dhamma* sees dependent origination.' "[17]

As evidenced by Sāriputta's quote of the Buddha, the teaching known in Pali as *paṭicca samuppāda* ("dependent origination" in the above) is central to the Buddha's *dhamma* (his teaching, his truth, his view of what is important). The two could even be said to be one and the same: dependent arising is the *dhamma*, the *dhamma* is dependent arising. The term as shown here, or in its other form as *paṭicca samuppanna*, is used in about three dozen *suttas*; its formulation in the classical twelve steps is repeated in several more *suttas*, and shorter varieties are also offered: nine links are the dominant form in the Dīgha Nikāya's *suttas*, and much shorter variants occur throughout the Sutta Piṭaka. Many explanations have been suggested for these differences, including the possibility that they represent corruptions (or that additional steps, bringing it up to twelve, are corruptions), or that they reflect the development of the Buddha's teaching methods as he practiced describing his insight to more people over the course of a lifetime. Any of these are possible, and I would add the possibility that he used the pieces he felt were most helpful in reaching his particular audience, so that on any given day he might only discuss the three or four steps he felt were critical to his message at that moment. He often introduced alternative directions that his chain of events could go in—for example, the one that leads to possessiveness and the taking up of sticks[18]—but

[16] Pali-English Dictionary Version 1.0, created by a group of monks in Sri Lanka, an electronic, public-domain edition based primarily on A.P. Buddhadatta Mahathera's Concise-Pali-English and English-Pali Dictionary, expanded with a series of corrections and additions.

[17] Sāriputta quoting the Buddha in MN 28.38 [pts M i 191] as translated by Bhikkhus Bodhi and Ñaṇamoli in The Middle Length Discourses of the Buddha (1995)

[18] DN 15 [pts D ii 58]

whatever the number of steps used and whatever terms he chose, the lesson always has the same underlying structure.

The most frequently cited description of the chain has twelve links, and it is this standardized list that makes the underlying structure of the teaching and its point clearest.

Classical Twelve Links and Their Usual Translations

1. *avijjā*—"ignorance"
2. *saṅkhārā*—"volitional formations"
3. *viññāṇa*—"consciousness"
4. *nāmarūpa*—"name-and-form"
5. *saḷāyatana*—"six senses"
6. *phassa*—"contact"
7. *vedanā*—"feeling"
8. *taṇhā*—"craving"
9. *upādāna*—"clinging"
10. *bhava*—"existence"
11. *jāti*—"birth"
12. *jarāmaraṇa*—"aging and death"

Interpretations of Dependent Arising

Paṭicca samuppāda has been interpreted in different ways over the course of history. The most popular interpretations have the twelve links describing the chain of events that keep us in *saṃsāra*, the wheel of a life filled with *dukkha*. There is the three-lives model championed by Buddhaghosa, with the early links representing a past life, in which actions create *karma* which has to be dealt with in the present life (in this model, the term *saṅkhāra* is effectively identical to *karma*); the middle portion describes behavior in the present life that is generating *karma*; and the final portion, beginning with birth (*jāti*), describes the next life that will deal with the consequences of this life's *karma*, which goes on to aging and death, only to continue the rounds.

In another view, the twelve steps are seen as describing one life, or at least all events as happening over the course of one life. In this understanding the steps are not perceived as completely linear, but birth is still literal birth, and death is of the body.

In both of the above interpretations, the final steps of dependent arising are conceived of as being about a literal birth and death, and its lessons are all about how we can break the cycle of *saṃsāra* to escape rebirth so that there will be no more aging and death.

Another popular view is that what is being described here is the moment by moment arising of our sense of self, so that dependent arising becomes a model of how consciousness is triggered by events, and we engage with them in a way that causes problems, and then we suffer for it. In this system, birth and death are interpreted as metaphors for the birth and death of a fleeting and reappearing sense of self.

This paper will suggest that all three systems are partially correct: dependent arising is about three lives and cycles of birth and death; it is describing one life in non-linear fashion; and it is showing us how fleeting moments give birth to an impermanent self that causes *dukkha*.

Problems With the Above Interpretations

There are, however, problems with these interpretations.

The models that assume that what is being described is literal cycles of rebirth find no support in the *suttas*, where the twelve links in the chain never go around again from the last link to the first. "Aging and death" is never described as the forerunner of "ignorance". Although dependent arising is often shown as part of Buddhist "Wheel of Life" imagery, *paṭicca samuppāda* is not described as a wheel or a cycle in any text. If it describes cycles of rebirth, it is odd that it never gets portrayed as a cycle; instead it goes from link one to twelve and stops[19]. It is also odd that if it is about the way *karma* from a past life brings about the present life, and the way our actions in this life create *karma* leading us into the next, the word for *karma* is not used in it, in its sense as intentional actions that carry future consequences.

The moment to moment interpretation of dependent arising finds some support in the *sutta* in which the Buddha describes the arising of consciousness with a metaphor of a monkey swinging from one branch of a tree to the next[20], but this model seems to me to have a problem in application: although my consciousness of what is happening in the moment does arise swiftly and can pass away just as fast, I do not perceive my sense of self vanishing and reappearing moment by moment.

[19] However, there is the extended liberative formula (found in the Upanisa Sutta SN 12.23 [pts S ii 30]), in which the last step is renamed *dukkha*, and that *dukkha* is shown as the inspiration to practice the Buddha's methods and break the chain; the step following *dukkha* is *saddha* (faith) and then the following steps describe the course of practice.

[20] SN 12.61 [pts S ii 95]

The idea of a fleeting self being born, suffering, and dying in rapid cycles belies our experience and the stubborn, persistent nature of the issues we deal with on a daily basis, as well as the fact that *dukkha* doesn't always come around that quickly in response to the sense of self that gives birth to it.

The concept of momentary consciousness is a good match for what modern science has recently been making clear to us, and it may be that the Buddha's description of how our minds work describes that process, yet—though the rapid arising and passing away of consciousness seems to be part of what is being pointed out in *paṭicca samuppāda*—thinking of it in terms of the "birth and death" of consciousness seems a bit of a stretch; that would seem to suggest that it is that very consciousness that experiences the suffering of aging and death.

For explanations of dependent arising to be satisfying, they need to describe what is readily visible to us when it is pointed out, since the Buddha suggests (in the quote above and elsewhere) that we can see it for ourselves, and his explanation is designed to help us see what goes wrong and why, to give us the power to fix the problem of *dukkha*. This is another problem with the models that see *paṭicca samuppāda* as describing cycles of rebirth: past and future lives related by *karma* are not actually visible to us, yet we should be able to see for ourselves what these twelve steps are modeling. (This paper does not argue that the Buddha didn't teach rebirth, though it does argue that rebirth was not the lesson the Buddha was conveying by teaching dependent arising.)

Professor Jurewicz's Playing With Fire

Many attempts have been made to decipher the structure of *paṭicca samuppāda*, with the hope of better clarifying what its point is, and many suggestions have been made in attempts to shed light on pieces or the whole. In a paper published in 2000, Joanna Jurewicz proposed that many of the terms used in dependent arising were referring to Vedic myths of creation. Her detailed analysis found correspondences between the Buddhist terms for the links and a variety of similar or related terms in the *Vedas*, the *Brāhmānas*, and the *Upaniṣads*. These works are thought to predate or be contemporaneous with the Buddha, so she reasoned that dependent arising may have been a refutation of many of the Vedic ideas discussed in the texts she worked on. The particular focus of her article was on the Vedic myth of creation, most famously associated with the deity Prajāpati (whose persona was later co-opted by Brahmā), whose role was that of First Man.

Professor Jurewicz's paper takes a look at both *paṭicca samuppāda* and the Vedic creation myth from the perspective of subject-object cognition, which (I would note) is central to much of Buddhism's consideration of duality—the perceived separation between self and other. She sets out to show that the Buddha "formulated the *pratītyasamutpāda* as a polemic against Vedic thought" and argues that "Through the identification of the creative process with the process that leads only to suffering, he rejected the Brāhmānic way of thinking in a truly spectacular way."[21] I have come to agree with her that this is indeed what he did; but this is not all that he did, as we shall see.

Starting with dependent arising's first step, "ignorance" (*avijjā*), she describes the beginning of the origin myth in which the *Ṛg Veda* tells us that at first there was neither existence nor non-existence, and that it was not possible to know anything beyond that. The unknowableness of the pre-creative state is precisely the point, because what the *Vedas* are all about, by definition, is knowledge. What is defined here from the Vedic point of view is not simply ignorance of what is, but the total inability to know anything—for there isn't anything to know. Jurewicz also points out that the term *avijjā* is not used for the matching part of the myth.

Next comes "the manifestation of the creative power of the Absolute" which, still in darkness, is unable to cognize anything. This state is not the same as the previous, unknowable "neither existence, nor non-existence", because something—the creative power—exists now, but a power is apparently all that it is. Something exists, so knowledge is now possible, but it is still ignorant, being in darkness, and because there is nothing else there. Jurewicz describes a later rendition of the same basic story in which "the Creator (*ātman*) in the form of man (*puruṣavidha*) realizes his own singularity". He is all that there is, and so the only potential subject for him to examine is his own self—he cannot be cognizant of anything else, for there is nothing else. In either version we can imagine that the First Man cannot have perceived himself to have form, because there was no space around him, and there were no active sense organs to be sensing anything; we are talking of pure awareness with nothing to be aware of except that it is aware, and that it is seeking something to be aware of.

Moving on to *saṅkhārā*, Jurewicz continues the creation story, describing the Creator as wishing for a second, so that he would have something to know. This second would be *ātman* as well, the Creator-

[21] *Journal of the Pali Text Society*, Volume 26 (2000), p. 78

ātman, but, effectively, divided. Jurewicz tells us that *saṅkhāra* derives from the root *saṃskṛ*, which in the relevant Vedic text is used to express the wish that will be fulfilled through building himself (*ātmānam*) "in the form of a fire altar, which is his body and the cosmos at the same time." The term *saṅkhāra*, then, would seem to represent both the desire for existence and the act that begins the process of bringing *ātman* into existence (though *ātman* is not actually completed until a later step).

The fire altar comes into the story through Prajāpati's "son" Agni, the fire deity/principle. Prajāpati's wish to duplicate himself through the creation of the fire altar makes Agni a sort of equivalent of the Creator, and at the same time Agni is the Creator's progeny, and the altar, and the world; all of these are equivalents of each other. Because Agni is fire, he is a hungry thing, which results in some drama. The main point to understand here is that just as Prajāpati was hungry to be able to know himself, though he had no means to do so, Agni/fire/the second self/*ātman* is also hungry. As Jurewicz points out[22], this is still the not-knowing—the "ignorance" (*avijjā*)—driving "the desire for *ātman*" (*saṅkhāra*).

In the instant of the creation of the second, there arises the subject-object split. The *ātman* remains hungry for knowledge, and what is doing the seeking is consciousness (*viññāṇa* in the Pali, *vijñāna* in Sanskrit); this is hungry to know itself, but it is having trouble doing so because it has no eyes or ears, in fact no senses, through which to know itself.

When Jurewicz brings us to *nāmarūpa* she notes that "the act of giving a name and form marks the final creation of the Creator's *ātman*." She relates *nāmarūpa* to naming ceremonies in which a father "confirmed his own identity" with his son and "by giving him a name he took him out of the unnamed, unshaped chaos and finally created him." This is what Prajāpati does in the final act of creation, when he shatters himself (his *ātman*) into a myriad of pieces to create the world and all its inhabitants. In this way the Creator, the Absolute, also known as Prajāpati (and later known as Brahmā), is in every one of us as *ātman*. Through this explosive act of creation, the world of the senses is gained: finally Prajāpati has the tools through which he can come to know himself. The only problem is that he has tucked *ātman* into so many different names-and-forms, that it is no longer recognizable;

22 ibid, p. 85. "It is worth noticing that in the very image of hunger the ideas of *avidyā* and of *saṃskarā* are present: hunger is both the lack of food and the desire to have it." And hunger is driven by (is a form and result of) the desire for existence.

from the Vedic point of view this is why none of us initially sees *ātman* in ourselves, and we have to work so hard to come to know the truth of things.

In the remainder of the article Jurewicz touches on many other possible links between the terms of the Buddha's *paṭicca samuppāda* and Vedic cosmology, but the above is enough to have laid the groundwork for pushing her work a little farther. I will refer to the same article later, when I draw attention to the number of ways in which the element of fire is referred to.

The Prajāpati Myth as How We Come To Be The Way We Are

It seems clear from the foregoing that the elements of the Vedic creation myth are a close fit for the first five links in the chain of dependent arising. We start from neither existence nor non-existence ("ignorance"; *avijjā*); the desire for existence ("volitional formations"; *saṅkhārā*); hungry awareness ("consciousness"; *viññāṇa*); splitting up into pieces ("name-and-form"; *nāmarūpa*); which provides the medium/tools through which we come to know ourselves ("the six senses"; *saḷāyatana*). This alone should give us more insight into what the Buddha was describing with *paṭicca samuppāda* .

Working with just the myth of All Creation arising from The First Man, we can guess that the Buddha was showing an audience familiar with the myth's conventions that this also describes who we are, and how we come to be. This description is being addressed on several levels simultaneously.

Ignorance

We come into the world ignorant of what came before us because, on a purely physical and personal level, we arrive ignorant of whether there was existence before us or not. This is likely to be the direct parallel the Prajāpati myth was originally addressing: that we are born ignorant of what came before is true in everyone's experience. In the Buddha's system we are also ignorant of what brings into being that which we mistake for *attā*. This is the ignorance that is at the heart of all our problems: we have this initial condition as part of our nature and we are not even aware of it. "Ignorance" (*avijjā*), then, has three levels: one addresses our actual state of ignorance at birth; on a second level, the physical is paralleled by the Prajāpati myth's state of unknowableness; and on a third level the Buddha is saying that we are born unaware of how we operate or why; in particular, we are ignorant of what brings our sense of self into being, ignorant of how we come to behave as we do.

Desire For The Self's Existence

Saṅkhāra also operates on three levels.

At the most basic, physical level, *saṅkhāra* seems to be talking about sex. As Richard Gombrich has pointed out[23], the word *kāma* (desire) is used in some texts to describe the volitional impulse.

The original myth may well have been making a complex play on our need for procreation. It is well known that the ancient authors of the *Vedas* were making parallels to how any individual comes into being when they described the explosion of Prajāpati into the multitude of forms: this is a reference to procreative ejaculation. In the Vedic way of seeing things, the desire for sons is tied into the desire for personal existence, both through the modeling of the creation of Agni out of his father, Prajāpati (only through this act does their shared *ātman* become complete), and through the necessity, in the current life, of having a son who will provide for his aging father, and continue to offer oblations that support him after death. All this makes the lust that leads to pregnancy a requirement for the "desire for existence" in the long term, and that lust ultimately turns nothingness into something.

The term *saṅkhāra* also suggests a pun, since its components could literally mean "making together", which is indeed how parents create a child.

The myth seems to be modelled on an understanding of how each of us comes to be: out of an unknowable state, through lust, born because of and into a continuum of the desire for existence. This gives us the first two levels of *saṅkhāra*. The third is the Buddha's point that the desire we have for a certain kind of existence (a desire that continues due to our ignorance of the depths of our desire for existence) drives us to the process of creating a self.

[23] "The Vedic 'Hymn of Creation' goes on to recount that somehow—inexplicably—a volitional impulse initiates the process of creation or evolution. This volitional impulse is there called *kāma*, the commonest word for 'desire'." Richard Gombrich, *What The Buddha Thought*, (2009) p. 134.

Consciousness

Because we are born wanting to exist, and the only way to satisfy that desire is, first, to come to exist, and then, second, to come to know that we exist through knowledge, the particular knowledge we need is of ourselves. It is the "wanting" that brings *ātman* (in the myth) or the sense that we have a self (in the Buddha's version) into existence. This is why *viññāṇa* is so hungry that it is always seeking, always craving something: it seeks to know itself; it needs the food of knowledge to survive. It started with desire for existence, so in order to be satisfied it must know itself, i.e., know that it exists.

Hungry consciousness is the source of the individuality of name-and-form because it divides the world up in order to know itself; and name-and-form feeds *viññāṇa*, consciousness, the food it seeks in order to continue existing/knowing that it exists.

To frame this in mundane terms, name-and-form does represent our tendency to split the world up into a dualistic view in which each of us is an individual (subject) and we see individual elements as outside us (objects); but more important than that is the way in which we tend to see some aspect of ourselves in everything we encounter: we sort things in terms of how they relate to us (are they useful; are they dangerous; are they like us in some way; are they too dissimilar). That tendency in our consciousness causes us to see the world not just in terms of subject-object dualities ("there is me, and there is what is outside of me") but to sort the world into what is mine, and what is antithetical to me ("there is what is helpful and I need that, and there is what is harmful and I should avoid that").

It is because we are seeking to know ourselves through everything we encounter that we see everything in terms of *nāmarūpa*; and it is because we are able to perceive, through *nāmarūpa*, that everything somehow relates to us, that *viññāṇa* continues. If we never saw anything in things around us that seemed to confirm that our theory that "we have a self" is true, hungry consciousness would starve to death. But because we do perceive that everything relates to us, *nāmarūpa* feeds *viññāṇa*.

Consciousness tucks itself into everything that captures its awareness; it sorts everything out with reference to itself; it creates an entire world (worldview) that revolves around—or "is"—its own self. The Vedic view would see the world and self as one and the same because that's just the way things are, but in the Buddha's system, one could say, we create our own world because we define the world in terms of ourselves. The world we create and the self we create are both constructs and complement each other.

Let me again summarize the multileveled references being made: the consciousness described here has its physical parallel in gestation, whether we think of it as "consciousness descending from a past life", as did those who believed in traditional rebirth in those days, or, in modern terms, of development of the abilities of the fetus. Its place in the origin myth is the spark of life resulting from a desire for existence that moves on to satisfy the original desire through knowledge. In the Buddha's system it represents the way our minds seek evidence of who we are (of our existence) through our senses, of the way we sort everything out with reference to how it relates to us.

Identification

Nāmarūpa, seen through the structure of the Prajāpati myth, represents both the existence which was created in the first steps finally taking on individuality, and the individual identities (to which we give names and which we perceive through their forms) of all the things that the created-one encounters. In the myth, the creator can't identify anything until he splits himself up. *Nāmarūpa* is, therefore both the individual (*ātman*, or what we mistake for *ātman*), and every individual thing in the world, because in the myth they are both one and the same thing. This is why *nāmarūpa* represents both the "birth" of that *ātman* as an individual, and all of the individuals he encounters in the world, which he will interpret as being (i.e., having reference to) himself. In the Buddha's lesson, *nāmarūpa* is addressing both the birth of our individuality, and the way we just naturally perceive everything "out there" to be part of us, to have reference to us.

Though we were, in a sense, born in the transition from the first step to the second, we are born again, into our sense of self, in *nāmarūpa*. This would be two births—which takes us back to Prof. Jurewicz's supposition that *nāmarūpa* also reflects a naming ceremony, in which the father gives the son his "final form", thus creating his *ātman* in the way Prajāpati completed his *ātman* with Agni. This presumably draws on the "twice-born" concept of Vedism—once from the mother's womb, and once again at an initiation rite. Real world: birth, then naming ceremony. Myth: existence, then splitting into name-and-form. Buddha: desire for that sense of self, followed by the way we identify the world as having to do with self, because it is out of that identification of our self with what we see around us that we create our sense of self, our second birth.

Direction of the Senses

In the Prajāpati myth, after "hungry desire for existence/knowledge" has split itself into individuals, it gains the senses, and uses those senses to seek to know itself. This is why the six senses and their objects (*saḷ-āyatana*) follow name-and-form (*nāmarūpa*): the six senses and their objects were created in one step; in the myth they are really one and the same thing, because Prajāpati's senses are gained through all those objects. The Buddha is describing for us the way in which our desire for self has us directing our senses in search of ourselves in everything around us. Thus we define everything in terms of the way it relates to us. Physical: ability to use the senses after we are born, so that we can encounter the world. Myth: Prajāpati's creations providing him with senses so he can know himself. Buddha: that we use our senses to meet hungry consciousness's desire for knowledge of the self. We actually direct our senses to identify that which supports our sense of self.

Bonds and Equivalences

The Vedic world view was built on an assumption of bonds (*bandhu*)—"relationships" softens what's being said too much between things—between us here on earth and the cosmic powers beyond this world, and between things in this world, for example between father and son. Another way of putting this was that it was all about equivalences; as in the Prajāpati myth, father and son were one and the same: they were equivalents of each other.

The Prajāpati myth in its place in Vedic ritual depends on these equivalences: our human lives are seen as being what they are because that's how things were set up when the First Man came into being, and the rituals modelled on those myths are a reenactment of them, not simply confirming them, but strengthening and keeping the connections in place.

The early steps of dependent arising define the conditions we start from, describe human nature as seen through the Vedic creation myth, and also describe what the Buddha sees: that we come into this world ignorant of any other way of being, or even of how we are; that we crave that sense of self, and so we create it; that our minds seek to know ourselves; and that in doing so we create ourselves through the way we identify with everything we encounter, which we do via our senses.

Saṅkhārā As Rituals

But this is not all that the Buddha had to say. With Professor Jurewicz's brilliant insights,[24] we are led to understand the origin myth, and to see how it helped the Buddha to describe how we come to be the way we are. She provides a clue to a deeper understanding of what *paṭicca samuppāda* describes when she ties the Buddha's term *saṅkhāra* to its Vedic roots, to Prajāpati's wish for a second, which would be acted upon through building his *ātman* as a fire altar. In the myth, *saṅkhāra* was a ritual that gave form to the wish for creation of the *ātman*, by creating an altar that was the equivalent of Prajāpati, of the world (for Prajāpati comprised the whole world at that point), and also of fire, Agni. The word *saṅkhāra*, in addition to perhaps being a pun on procreation (the "making together" of a child), here seems to reflect the perception that a real life event has the effect of "putting together" the *ātman*. That event is a social event, something people do together in communal rituals.

The *saṅkhāra* is a fire ritual; its tamer cousins are still enacted today in transformative *samskāra* rituals prescribed to mark moments of transition in the lives of high caste Hindus. Though not classed as a *samskāra* ritual, the biggest fire ritual of all, the Agnicayana, marked the completion of the transformation of *ātman*, the passage from this life grounded in the senses, to a world beyond. Both the *samskāra* rituals and the Agnicayana are rituals that have as a purpose the creation and/or perfection of the self to improve personal outcome after death.

In the life of a modern Hindu, the options seem to be either to be reborn (hopefully as a human, but that depends on one's *karma*), or, through the perfection of one's knowledge of *ātman* to become one with (as Jurewicz puts it) "the Absolute", also known as *brahman*.

Around the time when the Buddha lived, fire rituals were a central part of daily life. From the brahminical point of view, the highest class of people were the brahmins themselves. Some were officiating priests who performed rituals for others, and some were householders, but all would have a household fire and daily rituals. The warrior class and merchant classes also had household fires and small daily rituals, but the big, transformative rituals were conducted by specialist brahmin priests. In the brahminical texts as well as in the Buddhist *suttas*, these rituals are described as sacrifices. Sometimes animals were sacrificed, sometimes vegetable matter, or animal byproducts like clarified butter, but in the transformative rituals, like the Agnicayana, the thing sacri-

[24] I am most indebted to her for giving me the grounding in the myth and language needed to see the underlying structure.

ficed is considered to be the equivalent of the person who sponsors the ritual—*bandhu* again—and for this reason he is called the Sacrificer, because he sacrifices himself (his *ātman*) on that pyre, whether in the form of a goat during sacrifices in the normal course of his life, or with his own flesh and bones after death.

It is unlikely that anyone living in the Buddha's society would have been unaware of the spectacular and time-consuming Agnicayana ritual, or the funeral ritual that marked the transition from death to whatever "other world" the Sacrificer had been aiming at with rituals his whole life long, whether that be a world of ancestors, of particular gods, or union with *brahman*. The Vedic system was built on the assumption that the rites practiced throughout a lifetime, as well as keeping the gods, ancestors, and the universe nourished, enabled the Sacrificer to nourish his self, his *ātman*, in the same way—constantly building and perfecting himself and his world, in both the present world and the world he would inhabit after death. The concept was that during the ritual the Sacrificer died (he/his equivalent was what was being sacrificed), he made his way up to his world, and returned to earth a new man—literally (but, to our point of view, figuratively). Over the course of a lifetime of such rituals in which the *ātman* was perfected, he would "die" and "be reborn" many times.

The rituals that revolved around the perfection of the self seem to have been the model the Buddha used for dependent arising. This makes sense for many reasons.

First, the rituals will have been so well-known throughout society that, when using them as a model, there would have been no need to explain what was being referenced. It would make as little sense for the Buddha to stop and point out that rituals were his model as it would make sense for a modern manual on scheduling to stop to explain the days of the week and hours in the day. That the model was so familiar explains why we find no explicit references to its being the structure underlying the lessons. That there are no explanations of what metaphor the Buddha was using explains a lot of our confusion in interpreting the terms.

Second, in case anyone missed the point that he was modeling the teaching on a ritual, he named his second step with a word that may have been in long use as meaning "ritual" (*saṅkhāra*).

Third, these rituals were like workshops in which one created and perfected the *ātman* over the course of time. The Buddha, as we know, denies that there is any *ātman* to be found. What he is telling us all throughout his lectures is that we create that which we mistake for the self. So he agrees with the Vedic view to the extent that we are creating something, but he denies that what we create is what we think it is, or that it lasts. That's why he can use the model of the *saṅkhāra* rituals effectively to say, "Yes, it goes more or less the way you say it does, but with a few small differences...". What better way to both refute what is thought to be going on and to show that something else is happening, than to do it all in one structure?

Finally, the embedding of the Prajāpati creation myth at the beginning also points to the chain of events being modelled, at least in part, on the Agnicayana ritual, because the Prajāpati myth was what was being modelled in that ritual itself. The fire altar that is built for the Sacrificer is constructed in the way Prajāpati built his—in the shape of a bird—and the altar is conceived as the equivalent of the Sacrificer, and of the world. Prajāpati is also known as the First Sacrificer, because he sacrificed himself by shattering himself into all of creation, into the individuality of name-and-form, as his act of creation. The Sacrificer, through this ritual, is re-enacting Prajāpati's act of sacrifice, and creation of the world, and union with it, himself taking the role of Prajāpati.

Performance of the Ritual

If the links in the chain of dependent arising are modelled on the Agnicayana ritual and the *saṅkhāra* rituals of self-perfection, with the Prajāpati creation myth built into the early steps, the next question is: what is the structure underlying what follows *saḷāyatana*'s acquisition, i.e., the use of the senses?

What I suggest comes from our knowledge of what the portions from "contact" (*phassa*) through "clinging" (*upādāna*) describe. This is the portion of the chain which seems to be best understood and is certainly most widely agreed on: it describes how, upon contact with the world, we react to it. It describes what we do day in, day out, over and over again: we engage with something, we experience it as good/bad/indifferent, we react to that experience, then we make assumptions about it in terms of how it relates to us. This is us doing what our senses direct us to do: naming-and-forming, identifying everything that happens to us in terms of how it relates to us, how it serves us, how it helps build up and stabilize our sense of self. It is all the things we do hundreds of times each day. It is our rituals.

I would suggest that the use of the word *vedanā* here, derived from a root shared with the name the Vedic people gave to their vast corpus of secret knowledge—the *Vedas*—is no coincidence. The *Vedas* represent the knowledge and ritual lore most precious to those orchestrating the sacrifices that create and perfect the *ātman*, while *vedanā* describes what we "know" about what we experience: how it feels. The *Vedas* lay out the performance of rituals in microscopic detail, and in this portion of dependent arising, we have our rituals laid out in just that way: tiny step by tiny step: "Here is how we do it: we start with our knowledge of an experience, and we build on that." In addition, the altar that is at the center of the ritual fires is called the *vedi*—so this term might also be referring to that altar. Starting with the ritual tools of our senses, in the ritual arena of the sensual world, we perform these rituals over and over throughout our lives, building up *ātman*—or rather, what we mistake for *ātman*.

It is almost as if the Buddha were saying, "Yes, we build a self that is like fire through our rituals, but these are the details of the actual rituals that make it happen. This is the knowledge that is important, not what is in your *Vedas*."

In her paper, Joanna Jurewicz notes that some of the terms in this section also relate to fire, for example *taṇhā*, which is *tṛṣṇā* in Sanskrit:

> "The Buddha in his descriptions of *tṛṣṇā* very often refers to the image of fire. I think that the reason why he does so is not only because the metaphor of fire is particularly expressive, but also because something more lies behind it: here he is referring to the Vedic image of creation as performed by human subjects."[25]

The reference to fire here would be two-fold: it is touching on the creation of *ātman*/second self/Agni, and also on fire being central to Vedic rituals (the Agnicayana in particular). Jurewicz notes that *tṛṣṇā* also makes particular reference to fire's activity—to the insatiable nature of fire. This makes *taṇhā* not only fit the model of the Agnicayana, but the perfect word to describe what is happening in reality, the way our very natures burn for more of what we perceive as nourishing us, for the fuel of our experiences matching up what happens with how it relates to us.

Given that *upādāna* can mean fuel (as well as, according to Jurewicz, a cognitive activity comparable to burning fuel) we seem to have been given all the instructions needed to see the performance of the ritual: the tools of our senses, the arena of the world of the senses, the activities of contact, our *Vedas* via knowledge of how the experience feels,

[25] "Playing With Fire", *Journal of the Pali Text Society*, Volume 26 (2000), p. 95

the fire that wants to burn, and the fuel for that fire, the fuel of our attachment to these very rituals.

Results of the Rituals

The links after *upādāna* are "existence" (*bhava*), "birth" (*jāti*), and "aging and death" (*jarāmaraṇa*). They can be interpreted in the rebirth models as literal descriptions of a being coming into existence from a past life, where *bhava* is seen as the arrival of something like "unresolved past *karma*" into the womb; some interpretations express this as consciousness descending into the womb. This is easy to understand, since the descriptions given in the *suttas* of birth and aging and death all sound fairly literal.

But given the number of layers of meaning in all that has gone before, and given that the Buddha is denying that what ritualists believe is happening is what is actually happening, it would be quite odd for this last part to mean exactly what was believed to be the result of an actual ritual: rebirth of some sort. All along, the Buddha has been denying the obvious interpretation, and showing that the truth is something else entirely.

To help us see this, here's a quick recap of the pattern of layering: the opening makes references to the Prajāpati myth, and rituals based on it, and points out how we arrive in the world (ignorant) and what drives us to do what we do. It simultaneously describes the creation of *ātman* and denies that what we conceive as *ātman* is exactly as normally described. Instead of a being born out of a craving for knowledge of the self, this is a notion born out of ignorance about the self; it is not *ātman* but that which we mistake for *ātman*. The middle portion has references to familiar rituals well known to society; it uses terms which evoke the texts (*Vedas/vedanā*), and the fire (*taṇhā /upādāna*), but all the while is describing an entirely different set of rituals; it does not say "Here's your ritual" overtly, but obliquely. Why, then, would the final portion be the only part meant to be taken literally?

But if the last links are not actually about gestation, birth, aging, and death, what do they describe? The answer should lie in the direction of the whole: if dependent arising is, indeed, modelled on transformative fire rituals, ending with the funeral pyre, rites that (when they mark the end of an ideal life) work as transformative events in which the *ātman* reaches final perfection so that it can be born into its blissful next world, or rejoin the creative force, the Absolute, *brahman* and go to eternal bliss, then this final portion too must be modelled on that transformation. We've done the rituals, we've built the pyre, we've fed it fuel; will the *ātman* now be perfected, be transformed through *bhava* (which also means "becoming"—a translation more suited to transition), and then go to bliss? No, says the Buddha, in this step, what we perceive as the *ātman* that has been created and built up all along is perfected and born, but instead of going to bliss, it goes on to age and die, just as we are all born, age, and die; not to bliss, but to *dukkha*.

Reading The Suttas With This Interpretation

The language in the *suttas*—perhaps in part because of the layering of meaning that seems to have been a common practice in that culture[26]—can be interpreted in several ways. Historically, a case has been made that the Buddha frequently talked about literal rebirth as a fact of existence into which he had direct insight and which he even experienced for himself; there is a lot of evidence that can be offered to support that conclusion.

But if dependent arising was actually designed to refute current ideas about rituals, and the *ātman*, and the afterlife, and instead to point out what we can see for ourselves when we closely examine our own rituals (performed in ignorance), it seems unlikely that literal rebirth was the focal point of the teaching.

Questions concerning rebirth are not the only unresolved issues about dependent arising in the *suttas*. There have also been questions about how unusual sequences in various *suttas* fit with its classical order. Besides, there are related portions of the texts that remain downright inscrutable. If this interpretation is completely misguided, it should become obvious as we examine the *suttas* that we have a hard time making our theory fit the texts; the theory would make the *suttas* make less sense if it is mistaken. If, on the other hand, our theory can be shown to be consistent with most *suttas* on the subject, and answer some of the unresolved questions, perhaps it will be approved. Only time—and many people willing to put in the effort to study and debate the issue—will really tell.

The classic definition of each of the twelve steps in the Sutta Piṭaka is in MN 9. Sāriputta there expounds each link in answer to the question "What is right view?"[27] The wording is repeated again in SN 12.2

[26] See Joanna Jurewicz' "Fire and Cognition in the Rgveda", ISBN 978-83-7151-893-5 pub. Dom Wydawniczy ELIPSA

[27] Sāriputta starts the sutta with wholesomeness, nutriment, and the four noble truths,

(without crediting a speaker), and portions of it recur in various other *suttas* (for example birth, aging, and death are described, with more detail on sorrow, lamentation, despair and grief, in DN 22). Because it is the most detailed description of all twelve in one place, we can use it as an index to the whole set, and see how Sāriputta's explanations fit the theory, adding other *suttas* as needed. He starts his discourse at the end of the chain of events, with aging and death: this is a logical starting place because it is what each of us does when looking for a cause: we spot an effect, and look back for the components that were required to bring it about.[28]

Sutta Support

Death (*maraṇa*)

> "And what is aging and death?... The aging of beings in the various orders of beings, their old age, brokenness of teeth, greyness of hair, wrinkling of skin, decline of life, weakness of faculties—this is called aging. The passing of beings out of the various orders of beings, their passing away, dissolution, disappearance, dying, completion of time, dissolution of the aggregates, laying down of the body—this is called death."[29]

A conversation the Buddha once had with Baka the Brahmā shows that the last link in the chain of dependent arising is not about literal aging and death, despite the way the above makes it look at first glance. Here is Baka speaking, followed by the Buddha's answer [30]:

> "'... Now, good sir, this is permanent, this is everlasting, this is eternal, this is total, this is not subject to pass away;

does all twelve links, and ends with the taints. The *sutta* can be found beginning at [pts M i 46]. All translations of MN 9 cited here are by Bhikkhus Ñaṇamoli and Bodhi, from Wisdom Publication's Middle Length Discourses of the Buddha, (1995), unless otherwise stated.

[28] Richard Gombrich points out that in the Vinaya Piṭaka it is the discovery of *paṭiccasamuppāda* that is the Buddha's awakening. Gombrich then shares an insight provided by his friend: "... Hwang Soon-Il has very plausibly suggested that this may be the origin of the common Pali expression *yoniso manasa-kāra*. The dictionary translates this with such terms as 'proper attention'. But literally it means 'making in the mind according to origin', and that is just how the Buddha made his breakthrough." p.132 of *What the Buddha Thought*

[29] MN 9.22 [pts M i 49]

[30] MN 49.3-.4 translation by Bhikkhus Ñaṇamoli and Bodhi [pts M i 326]

> for this is where one is neither born nor ages nor dies nor passes away nor reappears (*upapajjati*), and beyond this there is no other escape.'
>
> "When this was said, I told Baka the Brahmā: 'The worthy Baka the Brahmā has lapsed into ignorance... in that he says of the impermanent that it is permanent, of the transient that it is everlasting, of the non-eternal that it is eternal, of the incomplete that it is total, of what is subject to pass away that it is not subject to pass away, of where one is born, ages, dies, passes away, and reappears, that here one is neither born nor ages nor dies nor passes away nor reappears; and when there is another escape beyond this, he says there is no other escape beyond this.'"

I would first note that I can find no sense in the Pali of Brahmā or the Buddha talking about a place—there is no "where" there—so this piece could be describing the perception that abiding with Brahmā was a permanent, eternal state (not a place), endless, no next state: no more rebirths. With his contention that within this state one still ages and dies, the Buddha seems to be saying that what is usually perceived as "abiding in the Brahmā-state" is actually a state of existence still in this world where aging and death continue.

The passage can certainly be interpreted as the Buddha saying that the Vedic highest goal of "abiding with Brahmā" instead puts one in a "place" (Brahmā's world, taking on a life which goes on for a long while) where one ages and dies and is reborn again, but having (perhaps purposefully) made no mention of place, the Pali doesn't seem to be denying a place and a life spent in it. Instead it seems to be discussing a state, which is presumably a happy one, since followers of this system are working hard to get there and stay there eternally; we can call it "a state of eternal bliss". Brahmā says it is without the usual pains of aging and death and being reborn again, probably because what Brahmā is describing is not literal life with him in a world, but the state of eternal bliss "in union with *brahman*". It is "total" and everlasting because it is the final rejoining with the Absolute that is being described here.

The reference to "reappearing" is usually seen as literal rebirth, but in the context of this new view that dependent arising is above all about *ātman* going through changes as a result of all our rituals, the reappearance referred to should be that which results from our frequent rituals. In those rituals the Sacrificer dies a virtual death each time, visits his other world, and returns to reappear (*upapajjati*) again. The last birth—following the final (actual) death—through the *bhava* of the death ritual, would not be thought of as *upapajjati* (which is why Baka says there will be no more of that). *Upapajjati* is what happens repeatedly in this life: we are born, grow up (age), join in the rituals, die, and reappear after the normal rituals; but not so after that last death marked by the rite of cremation.

Brahmā wants us to believe that at some point *ātman* gets to rest in eternal bliss, but the Buddha is saying *ātman* just returns to doing what we have always seen him doing, being modified by our rituals—not the Vedic rituals, but our rituals. It is not really *ātman* the Buddha is discussing here, it is whatever we mistake for *ātman*.

We keep changing as a result of our rituals (the ones that begin with *vedanā*) and when we get through the transition of *bhava* and come out the other side, as long as we are still creating that sense of *ātman*, it is still going to experience aging, sickness, and death, and go around again with the next change caused by our rituals. It is what passes for *ātman* that goes on the rounds, and it is that which the Buddha is identifying here as "impermanent, transient, non-eternal, incomplete, subject to pass away, born, aging, dying, passing away and reappearing."

In MN 1[31] the Buddha can be seen to address the way that the events described in dependent arising create something that "comes to be", and that it is this which ages and dies:

> ...the Tathagata, too, accomplished and fully enlightened, directly knows earth as earth. Having directly known earth as earth, he does not conceive [himself] as earth, he does not conceive [himself] in earth, he does not conceive [himself apart] from earth, he does not conceive earth to be 'mine', he does not delight (*abhinandati*) in earth. Why is that? Because he has understood that delight is the root of suffering, and that with being (*bhava*) [as condition] there is birth, and that for whatever has come to be there is ageing and death.

A traditional interpretation might suggest that "whatever has come to be" describes "every single thing that has come into existence" in which case the above is simply a statement about impermanence. Yes, it is about impermanence; but given the context of the paragraph, it also has to do with conceptions of the self. It is not about the impermanence of any old "whatever" but is, instead, about the impermanence

[31] MN 1.171 translated by Bhikkhus Ñaṇamoli and Bodhi [pts M i 6].

of that sense of self. If we look closely at the above we can see a mini-*paṭicca samuppāda* which goes from "delight" (a frequent synonym for *upādāna*), to *bhava* to birth to 'aging and death'. This means that if dependent arising is using a ritual that was thought to create and perfect *ātman* to describe the birth of something we mistake for *ātman*, then it is that false *ātman* which is what arises, and aging and death await it. In the example above, it is that sense of the self as to do with earth which arises from delight in earth, but MN 1 shows that in any way[32] we conceive that self, it is from that conception that the mistaken sense of self comes to be (is born), ages and dies.

This is why, when the Buddha was talking to Baka the Brahmā, he said that there was an escape beyond, and why he also repeatedly says that there is an unborn, unaging, undying, "beyond birth, aging, suffering, death". It is the false sense of self that he is describing as being born, aging, suffering, dying; so naturally, when he tells us we can rid ourselves of it, we would then be beyond that birth, aging, suffering and dying: we would no longer experience the *dukkha* that arises from our sense that we have a lasting self. And, I contend, that is the only *dukkha* the Buddha is ever talking about.

Aging (*jarā*)

As for the aging portion of *jarāmaraṇa*, MN 26[33] has this example of what is meant:

> "And what may be said to be subject to aging? Wife and children are subject to aging . . . sheep, fowl and pigs, elephants . . . gold and silver are subject to aging. These acquisitions (*upadhayo*) are subject to aging; and one who is tied to these things, infatuated with them . . . being himself subject to aging, seeks what is also subject to aging."

Here it is clear the Buddha is not really talking about an individual's own aging as the problem, and perhaps not even the aging of wives and children, sheep and fowl, our possessions, since "gold and silver" are described as aging, too, when, in the reality that concerns us, their aging is of no great importance, though they can of course be stolen from us. This means that in the piece above, "aging" is presented as a metaphor for impermanence, so we can interpret the section this way:

---

[32] I say that the sutta talks about "any way we conceive that self" by giving us what appears to be a comprehensive list of every way the self was conceived, in the Buddha's time, and denying all of them.

[33] Translation by Bhikkhus Ñaṇamoli and Bodhi [pts M i 162].

> "One who is himself impermanent is tied to these impermanent things, infatuated with them. Being himself subject to impermanence, he seeks what is also subject to impermanence."

The way it was phrased by the Buddha is far more poetic than my version, but either way it can be seen to say that we feel drawn to what is similar to us: we see our impermanent selves reflected in the impermanence of everything around us. This repeats the message of *nāmarūpa*, that we look for ourselves in things and find aspects of ourselves there, and we make those things part of ourselves. The use of the word "acquisitions" (*upadhayo*) seems likely to be wordplay relating the way we own things (*upadhi*) to the way we cling to them and make them part of ourselves (*upādānakkhandā*).

When the Buddha talks about the problem with gold and silver's aging, we can see that the real concern is not with an escape from aging, but with escaping from the *dukkha* that can result from aging. This makes aging a euphemism for all impermanent things. It is our infatuation with acquisitions (of things related to us in some way, of self) that are impermanent that is the problem, not the impermanence itself or even the things which are subject to impermanence. It is not aging that is the problem, it is the way we relate to things that age by making them part of our concept of self.

Both Aging And Death (*jarāmaraṇa*)

Sāriputta's classic description of *jarāmaraṇa*, quoted above, gets offered as proof that the Buddha was speaking about literal rebirth because this seems to be a literal description of aging and death—which of course it is:

> "And what is aging and death?. . . The aging of beings in the various orders of beings, their old age, brokenness of teeth, greyness of hair, wrinkling of skin, decline of life, weakness of faculties—this is called aging. The passing of beings out of the various orders of beings, their passing away, dissolution, disappearance, dying, completion of time, dissolution of the aggregates, laying down of the body—this is called death."

The Buddha is again making a point with this last step: that when what we think of as *ātman* goes through a transformation (*bhava*), it just reappears in the same old world in which it suffers through aging, sickness, and death; so, yes, the text is describing this step literally because that is literally what that which we mistake for self experiences. But what it experiences is not simply aging and death, it is the *dukkha* that, through conceptions of self, comes to overlay them.

Because with this last step the Buddha is talking about the opposite of bliss, and because the end product of the whole process of dependent arising is *dukkha*, aging-and-death can best be interpreted as a metonym for (or the equivalent of) *dukkha*.

In the extended, liberative *paṭicca samuppāda* found in SN 12.23 (the Upanisa Sutta), the usual chain is extended into the path to liberation, and the liberative part of the path there starts with "faith" (*saddha*), which has *dukkha* as its condition; but *dukkha* has "birth" (*jāti*) as its condition, and the whole chain regresses from there back to "ignorance" (*avijjā*) in the normal way. Missing from this chain is "aging and death" and *dukkha* stands in its place, so *jarāmaraṇa* is being given there as the precise equivalent of *dukkha*. If we see *paṭicca samuppāda* as modelled on rituals, then what "aging and death" really is, coming at the end of dependent arising, is the Buddha's way of saying that the results of all those repeated rituals is not bliss, but just "more of the same"[34]: it is *dukkha*, the opposite of bliss.

That what is meant by *jarāmaraṇa* is precisely *dukkha* is also clear in the description of one of the questions the Buddha asked himself that led him to his insight [35]:

> *pubbeva me, bhikkhave, sambodhā anabhisambuddhassa bodhisattasseva sato etad ahosi:–'kicchaṃ vatāyaṃ loko āpanno jāyati ca jīyati ca mīyati ca cavati ca upapajjati ca. atha ca panimassa dukkhassa nissaraṇaṃ nappajānāti jarāmaranassā.*
>
> "Bhikkhus, before my enlightenment, while I was still a bodhisatta, not yet fully enlightened, it occurred to me: 'Alas, this world[36] has fallen into trouble, in that it is born,

[34] When I say that "more of the same" is *dukkha*, I am not saying that the Buddha says that "life is *dukkha*", or even that the unenlightened life is *dukkha*. It is not all *dukkha*. The issue is just with the things we do with those rituals—when we are not doing "the usual stuff" life always has the potential to be wonderful. Our lives are a mix of doing things without quite understanding why we do them, things that are based on the desire for self the Buddha is describing, and doing things that aren't in that category—selfless things, for example, or simple, joyful things.

[35] SN 12.10(i) translated by Bhikkhu Bodhi [pts S ii 10].

[36] Also note the (to us) odd use of "the world" as something that can suffer—this seems to be a reflection of the Prajāpati myth, where self-is-world and world-is-self and

> ages, and dies, it passes away and is reborn, yet it does not understand the escape from this suffering [headed by] aging-and-death...'"

Although "headed by" has been inserted into the translation, the Pali actually presents the two terms *dukkha* and *jarāmaraṇa* as equivalents: "The many diverse kinds of suffering that are aging and death arise in the world..." or perhaps "The many diverse kinds of suffering that we call aging and death arise in the world..." It is possible that the phrase "aging and death" was a known metonym for all kinds of *dukkha*,[37] but at any rate, we can see here again that "aging and death" is just another way of saying *dukkha*.

In SN 12.35[38] the Buddha is specifically asked who it is that ages and dies, and his answer is dependent arising. By giving that answer he specifically points to that which is "born" through that process as being what experiences aging and death:

> "Venerable sir, what now is aging-and-death, and for whom is there aging-and-death?"
>
> "Not a valid question," the Blessed One said. "If one were to ask, 'Which aging & death? And whose is this aging & death?' and if one were to ask, 'Is aging & death one thing, and is this the aging & death of someone/something else?' both of them would have the same meaning, even though their words would differ ... From birth as a requisite condition comes aging & death."

The reason why the answer seems so obscure is that it cannot be made in terms of a person who is the result of a rebirth experiencing aging and death, because that is not what dependent arising is talking about. Through the lens of this interpretation, this is simply saying that "that which arises/is born" is that which experiences "aging and death"—which is just a metonym for *dukkha*.

Birth (*jāti*)

In MN 9, Sāriputta gives a detailed exposition on each of the links in the chain of events, and his description of "birth" (*jāti*) has long been

since they are equivalents they can be used interchangeably.

[37] If "aging and death" was a known metonym for *dukkha*, this might help make sense of the question, in the quote from SN 12.35 below, which mentions the question "Which 'aging and death'?"

[38] Translated by Bhikkhu Bodhi [pts S ii 61].

held up as a very strong piece of evidence that the Buddha was making it clear that there was rebirth and we were bound to its cycles, because it seemed that this piece could not be interpreted any other way:

> "And what is birth?. . . Whatever birth, taking birth, descent, coming-to-be, coming-forth, appearance of aggregates, & acquisition of [sense] spheres of the various beings in this or that group of beings, that is called birth."[39]

As translated, this is usually interpreted as literal birth (or, more accurately, as a rebirth). However, when viewed within the context of a dependent arising modelled on transformative rituals, it cannot be meant quite so literally. First of all, in the ritual setting, this "birth" would not generally be referring to a birth into an actual body at all, but into the world of one's ancestors, or perhaps bliss with Brahmā. Within the lesson it is offering, though, it should be addressing the same point as the conversation with Baka the Brahmā: not eternal bliss, just more of the same *dukkha*. The Buddha is simply saying that the rituals we perform do not cause *ātman* to go to bliss in another world, they cause what we mistake for *ātman* to keep reappearing in this one.

It is interesting that the "appearance of the aggregates" is mentioned as part of birth, since there is every indication that the Buddha perceived the troubles that we have through the creation of our problematic sense of self to start up at about the same time as does sexual lust[40], so those aggregates that fuel our mistaken sense that we have a self would not appear at birth, but long after. Those aggregates, however, would appear with each fresh rebirth of our false sense of self, so I would suggest that this is actually what is being described here: the birth and reappearance of that which is not self, here labeled as "a being".

Another way of looking at this particular definition—and, in fact, all of Sāriputta's descriptions in MN 9—is to see that he is not really defining what is happening as part of the process, so much as talking about a specific requirement for this moment to happen.

---

[39] Translation by Thanissaro Bhikkhu http://www.accesstoinsight.org/tipitaka/mn/mn.009.than.html

[40] For example in MN 38.28-29 [pts M i 266] , where he describes a boy's life from conception to maturity, and the clinging is not introduced until after he's gotten past the stage of playing tipcat and with toy ploughs; only when the strands of sensual pleasure kick in does the trouble begin.

A Note On Nutriment

In the Vedic cosmology there is a great deal of concern with food, with "nutriment". This is such a strong influence in the culture that the gods are described as being fed by our little selves there in their world, and the sacrifice offered in rituals is seen as ascending in the smoke to sustain the gods or forefathers, and the sacrificer is understood to be banking nutriment to make his stay up there in bliss last long[41]. Not surprisingly, given that the society was heavily involved in settling new lands and developing the science of agriculture, another popular analogy was to the growing of food. If each of these steps is looked at in terms of nutriment—as the very most basic "ground" of things needed for this step to happen—Sāriputta's descriptions not only make sense, they become a way of pointing out exactly what we need to look at to see the step occurring.

As we go through the remaining links in the chain of events, we can examine how this makes what's going on easier to spot, but for the moment let us keep the focus on "birth". It is clear that if there were no birth, ever, of any being anywhere, there could never arise any false-self or any *dukkha* resulting from the appearance of that mistaken sense of self. That makes "birth" the necessary "field" for that sense of self to grow in.[42] At the same time, we are also being asked to pay attention to how a particular sort of birth—the one that comes with the appearance of the aggregates—causes *dukkha*.

Literal birth is not the primary cause of *dukkha*. It is one of many component causes that are required for anything at all to happen, true, but it is just a field. Lots of good things come from the same field; there would be no life at all were it not for birth. But the acquisition of the aggregates is also pointed out as something for us to look at—so that we can see what is born from those ways in which we conceive of a self.[43] It is true that if we stop literal birth, *dukkha* stops, but so does all the good stuff that comes from the same field, so what is being addressed here is, as usual, multileveled: without birth, no birth of the

[41] Which is probably why the terms for merit and its rewards have their roots in the ripening of crops.

[42] It does not mean that what we need is to stop birth.

[43] We can also look at Sāriputta's analysis of aging and death in the same way: if there were no infirmity, no aging, no one ever died, there would be no food—no nutriment, no field—in which *dukkha* could grow. That there is such a thing as loss of abilities, and the things we are attached to do sicken and die and pass away—literally or metaphorically, as with silver and gold—that provides the field, the nutriment, a ground for us to grow *dukkha*. The literal is just the ground—we have to plant the seeds for something to grow.

mistaken sense of self; the same is true without the appearance of the aggregates. The thing that is the proximate cause, the thing that goes to the heart of the trouble and gives us no goodness at all, that is the part that needs to be stopped, not the furthest cause, the one that also gives good stuff.

Becoming (*bhava*)

The word *bhava* has long been a problem for translators. It often gets translated as "existence" or "being", which represents a steady state (except in phrases like "coming into existence"). Translating it as a state one is in and stays in may be causing confusion.

As part of a process like dependent arising, it is clearly a process itself, and since it marks the transition from one state (less pure *ātman*) to a different state (purer *ātman*), the other common translation of "becoming" suits it better. In its place before "birth" it can be seen as a sort of gestation, a moment or a period of change from one state to another.

The classic definition of "becoming" is found at MN 9.28[44]. When Sāriputta is asked "What is becoming?" his answer is:

> *tayome, āvuso, bhavā — kāmabhavo, rūpabhavo, arūpabhavo.*
>
> "There are these three kinds of being: sense-sphere being, fine-material being, and immaterial being."

Kāmabhava should not be too hard to understand. It is usually translated in terms of sensual pleasures, and though I tend to think it means more than that[45], the usual translation should be sufficient in this quote. The other two terms, *rūpa* and *arūpa*, have been variously translated over the years but "form" (here "fine-material") and "formless" ("immaterial") are currently popular. How these words are interpreted by modern translators seems to vary, but the context is dependent arising's discussion of how we create our sense of self—and we are not simply talking about the self we have in this moment, but also about mistaken views of what an eternal, ongoing "self" (*ātman*) would consist of and would be after death. So the point here may

[44] [pts M i 50]

[45] I suggest that it is all sense information that we cling to as relating to self, not just the "sensual pleasures"; it represents all the problematic things we do even when we don't have a philosophy we cling to, because even non-conceptual impressions that we have a self begin with incoming sensual information.

concern one's habitual attitude: whether one thinks little about where or whether one will be reborn and just lives for the moment through the senses (*kāma*); or one believes in being reborn into the world of the ancestors, where one takes "form" (*rūpa*) and hangs out munching on meritorious supplies; or one becomes one with *brahman* "with no form" (*arūpa*) at all. This interpretation remains speculative, and deserves a paper of its own, but the present paper will continue noting the ways it fits into the detailed descriptions of *paṭicca samuppāda*.

Sāriputta's description again appears to point to a field, in this case the field in which *bhava* takes its nourishment: how we conceive of the self (i.e., the most popular ways in those days). If we were not busy perceiving our self as one of those sorts of being, we would not be creating the sense of self that gets born in the next step. In other words, without our conviction that we are in a world in which [pick your worldview] is the cosmic order and the consequent belief that we will become [pick the outcome of that worldview] after death, a sense of self that conforms to that view could not possibly be born in the next step.

If *bhava* is taken as "becoming"—that is, as a transition from an old sense of self to a newly upgraded version of a false self—the following translation stops being about ending rebirth/a final end to any existence at all:

> "Friend, though I have clearly seen as it really is with correct wisdom, *Nibbana* is the cessation of existence, I am not an arahant, one whose taints are destroyed."[46]

It would instead be about simply ending that sense of having a lasting self, so it becomes "Nibbana is the cessation of becoming"—where "becoming" represents a renewed sense of self, "becoming a fresh set of the aggregates" caused by clinging (*upādānakkhandā*). *Nibbana* could not have been the cessation of plain old existence at any rate, or it would be annihilation, and would indeed have been instantaneous upon awakening; so it has to be the cessation of the existence of something we've been trying to get rid of, and that would be our conceptions of a lasting self.

The view that the three "becomings" are the possible conceptions of *ātman*'s place in the universe is also supported by MN 9's[47] explanation of the origin of *dukkha*:

[46] SN 12.68 translated by Bhikkhu Bodhi [pts S ii 118].
[47] MN 9.16 [pts M i 48].

> And what is the origin of suffering? It is craving (*taṇhā*), which brings renewal of being (*ponobbhavikā*), is accompanied by delight and lust, and delights in this and that; it is craving for sensual pleasures (*kāmataṇhā*), craving for being (*bhavataṇhā*), and craving for non-being (*vibhavataṇhā*). This is called the origin of suffering.

Here we have craving as three types, *kāma* again, and *bhava*, as well as *vibhava*. If my hypothesis is right, "regular old *bhava*-type *taṇhā*" could match the *rūpabhava* mentioned above, where it would be the culture's majority understanding of *karma* and birth into an "other world" of form after death; and *vibhava* would correspond to *arūpabhava*, where *vibhava* would mean something "beyond becoming" or "beyond form" or "other than form" (i.e. "formless").

Fuel (*upādāna*)

Upādāna's succinct definition (as found in MN 9) has it as concerned with four things in particular: *kāmupadanaṃ*, *diṭṭhupadanaṃ*, *sīlabbatupadanaṃ*, and *attavādupadanaṃ*. As with *bhava*, above, the list starts with *kāma*, then seems to head off in a different direction, since there are four items listed here rather than three. The first (new) entry is *diṭṭhi*, which is views of/about things. *Diṭṭhi* is views which have an effect, as opposed to detached opinions. The next two items, *sīlabbatupadanaṃ*and *attavādupadanaṃ*, on examination, turn out to be views as well, the former being how people cling to their "rites and rituals" (which is what the whole of dependent arising is discussing!) and the latter views about the self (ditto!). In a sense, *diṭṭhi* seems to be central to this link—the views we have about what makes us what we are—and the other three are simply the commonest examples of the things that people held strong opinions about, the ones that get them the most *dukkha*: sensuality, ritualism, and views of the self.

When Dhammadinna answers a question about whether *upādāna* is equivalent to the *khandhā* in *upadanakkhandā*, or is separate from it, the nun's answer is "neither". She then explains what *upādāna* is:

> "It is the desire and lust in regard to the five aggregates affected by clinging that is the clinging there."[48]

This means that *upādāna* is the desire and lust that form around the sense of self, the sense of what constitutes the self, including all the

[48] MN 44.7 translated by Bhikkhus Ñaṇamoli and Bodhi [pts M i 300].

important issues that that brings up in Vedic society (i.e. where one goes after the breakup of the body). It is the desire and lust for whatever sense of self we have at the moment, whether it is about *kāma*, or *sīlabbata*, or *attavāda*, or some other *diṭṭhi* (view). The aggregates are those points we cling to that are specifically generated by (affected by) *upādāna*, the fuel for our sense of self, the fuel of opinions.

Sāriputta's description again points out the field that causes or allows the clinging to grow: It is views, views about right behaviour and about rituals, views about our sensual needs, views about the self. Without these views, there would be no fuel for the ritual fires in which we create our sense of self, so they are what we need to understand and discard.

Thirst (*taṇhā*)

Craving (thirst) we have already mentioned, when covering *bhava*, as being about *kāma*, *bhava*, and *vibhava*. So it also relates to *saṅkhāra*, because *saṅkhārā* are, in the original sense, craving for existence, for coming into existence (which would be *bhava*) as well as for continuing to exist (*bhava* as ongoing process). Here the Buddha could be talking about the ways we conceive of ourselves: as simple, sensual creatures (the ones to whom things just happen, with no particular cause); or as creatures who pass through "becoming" into the world of form (*rūpa*); or through *vibhava*'s "beyond becoming" into the formless (*arūpa*).

In the world that created the model for dependent arising, the Sacrificer performed rituals to gain and perfect knowledge of the self that makes these preferred outcomes happen; meanwhile, in the parallel lesson the Buddha is providing us with, we tend to confirm our preconceptions through our daily rituals, by relating them to our sense of self.

This is why in MN 9[49] craving also gets described in terms of craving for the objects of the senses.

> "There are these six classes of craving: craving for forms, craving for sounds, craving for odours, craving for flavours, craving for tangibles, craving for mind-objects."

It is through the senses that we build up the experiences we base our views (*upādāna*) on. The views then act as fuel for the fire of transition to our sense of self. When Sāriputta explains *taṇhā* in terms

[49] MN 9.38 [pts M i 510]

of the senses, he is not really explaining what *taṇhā* is or does, so much as pointing out the field in which it operates. When we are looking for that thirst for our sense of self in operation, we need to look specifically at the senses as they react to good feeling, bad feeling and neutral feeling; so Sāriputta is asking us to attend to that feeling of "I want more" or "I want to get away from it" that arises in response to sensory information.

Feeling (*vedanā*)

> "And what is feeling, what is the origin of feeling, what is the cessation of feeling, what is the way leading to the cessation of feeling? There are these six classes of feeling: feeling born of eye-contact, feeling born of ear-contact . . . feeling born of mind-contact."[50]

Sāriputta's explanation of feeling in MN 9 is a simple one: feeling derives from the senses. His formulation is modelled on the classic description of the noble truths: what it is, its origin, cessation, and the way to its cessation[51]. Describing feeling as originating in the senses is entirely logical, though on the surface this tells us little about the part it plays in the process being described. Contact with a sense is the most fundamental nutriment for feeling to arise; it has to be there for us to see what is being pointed out. We need to pay attention to those senses when they make contact.

Dhammadinna, on the other hand[52], talks of feeling in terms of pleasant, painful, and neither of those. What is most useful in her discussion is that she then describes what underlying tendencies relate to these three kinds of feeling: lust (*rāga*) underlies pleasant feeling, aversion (*paṭigha*) underlies the unpleasant, and ignorance (*avijjā*) underlies the things we feel as neither pleasant nor unpleasant; we seem to dismiss the things we have no particular feeling about as if they did not matter at all because, of course, "they have nothing to do with me".

---

[50] MN 9.42 [pts M i 51]

[51] In fact, all the descriptions in MN 9 are framed in terms of that same formula for the Four Noble Truths. In this way we can see that in some sense every step of dependent arising is actually *dukkha*, and that is because its end-product is *dukkha*: what dependent arising describes is *dukkha* and its origin. Or it can be seen as describing the arising of a false sense of self and its origin (the two are the same). Or really, given the conversation with Baka the Brahmā, it describes impermanence, for which we should be grateful: because of impermanence, dependent arising also describes the end of *dukkha* and the way to end it.

[52] In MN 44 [pts M i 302]

So we can easily see that the type of feeling determines the reaction to it (which is a form of *taṇhā*).

Contact (*phassa*)

Contact's origin, as described by Sāriputta in MN 9[53], is also simply located in the senses, because he is still describing where we look, in this case for contact.

> "There are six classes of contact: eye-contact, ear-. . . nose- . . . tongue-. . . body-. . . mind-contact."

Once again, what he describes is the food that sustains the process, and where to look to see it for ourselves. When Mahā Kaccāna explains some cryptic remarks the Buddha has made about the source of perceptions, he begins by describing what makes up contact:

> "Dependent on the eye and forms, eye-consciousness arises. The meeting of the three is contact. With contact as condition, there is feeling. What one feels, that one perceives."[54]

Kaccāna's explanation, like Sāriputta's, is anchored in the senses, which is natural, since the senses themselves are the step just before this one. The senses and their objects—i.e., the activation of the senses—are required for contact, and the object of the senses is actually found in the step one further back, in *nāmarūpa*, where *rūpa* not only means "form", but is the individuation of things in such a way that each thing relates to us, so that we find ourselves in it. We are not just talking about any contact, but contact of a specific type, contact that satisfies the particular desire for confirmation of the self.

Kaccāna's statement goes back further still, for it relates to consciousness. Why would that be? Because it is hungry consciousness that is doing the seeking, that is directing the senses to look for nourishment, and it is that particular instance of consciousness that will cling to, or avoid, or ignore what it finds, depending on the feeling that arises from the contact. It is only when contact has encountered a suitable object that the sense's awareness is fed, nourished, and arises—the tiny cycle of seeking for self and finding self has been completed.

We can see it this way: consciousness is not fulfilled—does not become complete—until it has something to be conscious of, and that

[53] MN 9.46 [pts M i 52]
[54] MN 18.16 translated by Bhikkhus Ñaṇamoli and Bodhi [pts M i 111]

"something" must be specifically what it is looking for; nothing else will satisfy it and make it complete. Driven by *saṅkhārā*, consciousness seeks the self. It is hungry but it is not real (not active, not sustained) until it has been fed. So when the eye meets a form, if that form confirms self, eye-consciousness now exists, because it has been nourished. That is what contact consists of: a moment when all the conditions of the drive to find the self have been met. Then feeling arises; feeling, which is knowledge of the experience (*vedanā*, our version of the ritual *Vedas*) comes to be, and then one can perceive both the self and the confirmation of the self in the world.

In Kaccāna's statement, there is implied the whole cycle of dependent arising up to the moment when the sense of self is about to be conceived: the eye-consciousness, finding satisfaction in contact through the eye with forms, has been driven to do this by the desire for existence that is *saṅkhāra*, and that is operating only because of ignorance. It is seeking confirmation of the self in the world because of the perception of name-and-form—the expectation that aspects of self will be found in the world around us, so the senses are directed to look for confirmation, and when contact of the right sort is made, the feeling that results feeds our perception of self.

Direction of the Senses (*saḷāyatana*)

The word *saḷāyatana* breaks down into six (*saḷ*) *āyatana*, and is usually translated as "the six sense bases". This is certainly what's being addressed, as in Sāriputta's[55] explanation of what it is:

> "And what is the sixfold base. . . ? There are these six bases: the eye-base, ear- . . . nose- . . . tongue- . . . body- . . . mind-base."

But, as usual, what is missing here is any sense of how the "base" fits into the process, what it does, what its function is. When *āyatana* is simply translated as "base" or "sphere" or "world of" we understand that it represents a cause (base) and is part of a creation (sphere/world), but there is no clear sense of why it is there beyond providing fodder for contact.

Other definitions of *āyatana*, found in PED, may make more sense:

> 1. stretch, extent, reach. . . 2. exertion, doing, working, practice performance. . .

[55] MN 9.50 [pts M i 52].

If the word is seen in an active sense, rather than as a passive recipient, it is a sense that is stretching out, extending, reaching, exerting itself. Then it becomes clearer that this refers to our senses driven to seek what *saṅkhārā* and consciousness are demanding we look for: ourselves and aspects of ourselves, through contact with the world.

The field for what is happening is the hungry senses, and that is therefore what we need to pay attention to. If we watch those senses we will notice how they are seeking something. They are the base from which the process of seeking for the self is able to act at this point in the chain.

Identification (*nāmarūpa*)

The most concise description of what "name-and-form" (*nāmarūpa*) is, as a link in dependent arising, comes again from Sāriputta[56].

> "And what is mentality-materiality? . . . Feeling, perception, volition, contact, and attention—these are called mentality. The four great elements and the material form derived from the four great elements—these are called materiality. So this mentality and this materiality are what is called mentality-materiality."

Again we have a description that appears to be straightforward and literal. If we take *nāma* ("name" or "mentality") to mean "mental processing" and *rūpa* ("form" or "materiality") to be just the physical, then what's being described is the body-mind duality. Doesn't it seem odd for the Buddha to say that this is what is real, what is happening? That there is this split—a mind and a body? This possible misinterpretation may come from the assumption that these descriptions say all that there is to say about each item and that they should be interpreted as absolutely literal descriptions of the link. However, that is apparently not all that is going on here. The pattern of his descriptions indicates that Sāriputta's definitions may not be fully delineating what part each link in the chain plays in quite the way we would.

For name-and-form to do its identifying, there does have to be a mind that is doing the processing: feeling, perceiving, intending, making contact, and paying attention; and there does have to be a material body functioning for this step to occur. Just as in the next step, active senses are required, and in the next, those active senses have to make

[56] In MN 9.54 [pts M i 53].

contact, and so on, right up to the way in which, for a sense of self to come into existence, there has to be a literal birth, and for *dukkha* to happen, there has to be food for it, too: aging, sorrow, despair, broken teeth, and death, because those are the things we make *dukkha* out of. Just so, the activities of *nāmarūpa* (feeling, perceiving, choosing, making contact, attending to the objects of our senses) require that we have name-and-form ourselves, and that the things we encounter in the world have it too.

Sāriputta seems to be asking us to pay attention to these to see what is going on in this step: notice the mental processing we do: notice how we see something (perceive it) through its form (*rūpa*) and we define it verbally (name it, *nāma*).

Given the background of the term *nāmarūpa* in the Prajāpati myth, and given this step's place in the ritual reenactment of that myth, it should go without saying that the defining we are doing in this step is finding ourselves in the myriad names and forms around us. This is why, in so many *suttas*, the Buddha points out that sometimes when we see something outside us, we say of it, "This is me, this is mine, this I am."

This interpretation is consistent with what we find in the Dīgha Nikāya's full treatment of *paṭicca samuppāda*, a text that has been a little bit muddy in interpretation in the past. A look at it through the lens of this theory of dependent arising makes it a little bit clearer.

Here is its description of *nāmarūpa* [57]:

> "From name-&-form as a requisite condition comes contact. Thus it has been said. And this is the way to understand how, from name-&-form as a requisite condition comes contact. If the qualities, traits, themes, & indicators by which there is a description of name-group (mental activity) (*nāmakāye*) were all absent, would designation-contact (*adhivacana samphasso*) with regard to the form-group (the physical properties) (*rūpakāye*) be discerned?"
>
> "No, lord."

It seems we are talking about how we define things based on their form. Here's my grammatically less accurate but I hope more intelligible translation of the same thing:

[57] Translated by Thanissaro Bhikkhu, http://www.accesstoinsight.org/tipitaka/dn/dn.15.0.than.html [pts D ii 62]

> "If the qualities, attributes, signs, and indicators by which we categorize things were not recalled when we make contact with something, would assigning special terms based on physical grouping be possible?"

In other words, if we had no definitions by which we categorize things based on the forms they take, would we know what they were by their forms? We couldn't.

Note that the word translated above as "designation" (*adhivacana*) carries a connotation of connections made between one sense of something and another. For example, in MN 5.9[58] it is used to express that when the term "blemish" is used, what is actually meant is "unskillful wishes", and in MN 19.26[59] it gets repeated use in matching metaphors to their real meanings.

With that in mind, the sentence above can be interpreted to say that because we already have in mind that certain physical characteristics of things connect to a particular meaning, when we see those characteristics, we categorize them that way; in the absence of those preconceived notions, we would not connect to forms in that way. That this is the point being made becomes clearer when we look at the next portion's reversal of the above, reflecting the pattern the first sentence established:

> "If the permutations, signs, themes, and indicators by which there is a description of form-group (*rūpakāye*) were all absent, would resistance-contact (*paṭighasamphasso*) with regard to the name-group (*nāmakāye*) be discerned?"
>
> "No, lord."

The above reverses what's being considered. Here the question seems to be: If we perceived a physical object as indistinguishable from every other object—if all the signs were missing—would we reject it? The unspoken part of this question—unspoken because knowledge of the mythology of the day is assumed—makes the sentence end: ". . . would we reject it as being too different from us?"

These considerations are part of the Prajāpati myth, which has two particular variations. In one of them the division of the Creator (so that he can seek himself) results in many diverse forms. This was the more popular version, in which the sense of self is lost in diversity. In the reverse variant of the tale, what is created is so uniform that there is no

[58] Translated by Bhikkhus Ñaṇamoli and Bodhi [pts M i 27]

[59] Translated by Bhikkhus Ñaṇamoli and Bodhi [pts M i 118]

way to distinguish self from other. When seen through the lens of the Prajāpati myths, in the first question Ananda is being asked: if the first case were true, if there were a zillion individuals and no two apparently alike, but we didn't have categories into which to sort things, would we be able to feel kinship with them, would we mistake them for self? And the second question is: if we could not distinguish between one form and another, including between ourselves and everything around us, would we reject things as alien?

Recognizing the two questions as having the Prajāpati myth as their unspoken, underlying source, makes the point clear: It is because we have already decided that the world has meaning that we behave as we do: accepting kinship with what is like us—and deeming those things necessary—and rejecting what is too different from us—and avoiding it.

> "If the permutations, signs, themes, and indicators by which there is a description of name-group and form-group were all absent, would designation-contact or resistance-contact be discerned?"
>
> "No, lord."
>
> "Thus this is a cause, this is a reason, this is an origination, this is a requisite condition for contact, i.e., name-and-form."

Contact, in DN 15's formulation of dependent arising, quoted above, follows from name-and-form, (the senses are skipped in this version) and it seems the outcome of that contact is being shaded into this definition: We come to know ourselves through contact, and we already have a tendency toward seeing ourselves as similar to or different from whatever we encounter. It is because we put things into categories, and because things have distinguishable forms, that we are able to do this. This means that *nāmarūpa*'s field is not simply that we must have a mind and body capable of making distinctions, but that there must be individuals with distinctly separate forms which we can use as the basis of our definitions. Both of these are the fields in which what we are doing in this step can flourish. We are being asked to notice the ways in which we relate to things through their names and forms.

Consciousness (*viññāṇa*)

> "'From consciousness as a requisite condition comes name-and-form.' . . . If consciousness were not to descend into the

mother's womb, would name-and-form take shape in the womb? "

"No, lord."

"If, after descending into the womb, consciousness were to depart, would name-and-form be produced for this world?"

"No, lord."

"If the consciousness of the young boy or girl were to be cut off, would name-and-form ripen, grow, and reach maturity[60]?"

"No, lord."

"Thus this is a cause, this is a reason, this is an origination, this is a requisite condition for name-and-form, i.e., consciousness."[61]

Here is another description that seems just too literal to interpret as meaning anything other than "the consciousness we are talking about is the one that arrives because of conception." Yet if we look at it as speaking to the requirement for this step to happen—in the same way that Sāriputta's descriptions of all that we've covered before stipulate what is necessary for each step to occur, rather than describe the process itself—it makes sense. The consciousness that arises due to our need to know that we exist, the consciousness that brings what we think is *ātman* into existence, does indeed require what we usually call consciousness, the mental-processing ability that was nurtured in a womb, had the chance to survive childhood, and matured (ripened) into the separate individuality designated by *nāmarūpa*. That general consciousness—our ability to think at all—is necessary for this step to happen. Meanwhile, there is ignorance-consciousness, *saṅkhāra*-consciousness, the self-seeking consciousness which is the thing we need to really take notice of.

The Prajāpati myth tells us that our desire for existence, our hungry consciousness, causes the birth of name-and-form; and the Buddha

60 Note that a young boy or girl does not have fully mature name-and-form—this matches with *nāmarūpa* being a reference to the point in their lives when youths are given the rites of passage to enter society as fully responsible members, and is also a reminder that, in the Buddha's system, the process being described doesn't begin before a certain level of maturity. For brahmin males, this point came long before puberty.

61 DN 15 Translated by Thanissaro Bhikkhu, http://www.accesstoinsight.org/tipitaka/dn/dn.15.0.than.html [pts D ii 63]

tells us the same: that we divide up the world with reference to ourselves, just as Prajāpati did in the myth. Both kinds of consciousness are needed and described, just as both kinds of birth are needed and described.

> "'From name-and-form as a requisite condition comes consciousness.' ... If consciousness were not to gain a foothold in name-and-form, would a coming-into-play of the origination of birth, aging, death, and stress in the future be discerned?"
>
> "No, lord."

It is easy to read the above on the fundamental, physical level as saying that if we did not have consciousness, we could not become individuals recognizable by our names and forms, and so we would not be born, age, die, or ever suffer stress; that is both clear and true. But it is also saying that if, in our desire to know ourselves, we did not divide the world up with our definitions, in ways that sort it out with reference to ourselves, we would not feed the consciousness that gives birth to that which we mistake for *ātman*, nor would that which arises suffer from aging and death, because it would not, in the future, come to exist. Both are true, and the condition defined by the former meaning is also necessary for the condition defined by the latter meaning to arise: we must have general consciousness existing in our individual form for the specific consciousness to seek and find itself in the things we identify as having to do with self.

> "This is the extent to which there is birth, aging, death, passing away, and re-arising. This is the extent to which there are means of designation, expression, and delineation. This is the extent to which the sphere of discernment extends, the extent to which the cycle revolves for the manifesting (discernibility) of this world—i.e., name-and-form together with consciousness."

To the extent that we use our definitions to delineate the world, to that extent will what we mistake for *ātman* be born, age, die, pass away, and re-arise, and to that extent will the world as we know it, as we define it, continue, because name-and-form and consciousness feed each other. In the final analysis, name-and-form is the field that feeds consciousness.

Saṅkhārā (saṅkhārā)

Sāriputta once again gives us directions: what to pay attention to in order to see *saṅkhārā* and what they do:

> "And what are formations? ... There are these three kinds of formations: the bodily formation, the verbal formation, the mental formation."[62]

This translation might be easier to understand if we see "formations" as "rituals". Look at the rituals we perform with our bodies, with our words and with our minds. What are our habits, what unexamined tendencies do we have, what things do we do without thinking much about them? These things are the fodder for our sense of self, they are the field in which it all happens.

> "And how, bhikkhus, should one know, how should one see, for the immediate destruction of the taints to occur? Here, bhikkhus, the uninstructed worldling ... regards form as self. That regarding, bhikkhus, is a formation (*saṃkhāro*). That formation—what is its source, what is its origin, from what is it born and produced? When the uninstructed worldling is contacted by a feeling born of ignorance-contact, craving (*taṇhā*) arises; thence that formation is born."[63]

The sort of contact that causes trouble for the worldling is that particular form of contact that has a particular sort of ignorance as its first cause. Ignorance-contact isn't about just any kind of contact; it has nothing to do with contact that doesn't make reference to our sense of self. It is the contact generated by the set of "givens" that is covered by the origin myth's portion at the beginning of *paṭicca samuppāda*.

This *sutta* is saying that *saṅkhārā* have as their source the kind of ignorance-contact that result in feelings that we relate to self. *Saṅkhārā* as the things we do, represent our craving for existence being fed what it hungers for: contact with what the senses are directed to look for. And this results in actions (habits, rituals) that bring that sense of self into visible existence.

Three things meet to make contact: the senses, their objects, and sense-consciousness. The moment of contact brings hungry sense-consciousness to completion by feeding it what it needs, making sense-

62 MN 9.62 [pts M ii 54]

63 SN 22.81 translated by Bhikkhu Bodhi, *The Connected Discourses of the Buddha* (2000), [pts S iii 96]

consciousness seem to arise out of sequence. In the same way, *saṅkhāra*'s circuit is completed only when an experience feeds it what it seeks.

The *saṅkhāra* in the above can be understood as the equivalent of "that which arises", of our mistaken sense of a lasting self, because it is "the desire for existence" given support by events. It is, one could say, that desire taking form as action. It then stands in for all that follows, which is why the rest of the quote above reads:

> "Thus, bhikkhus, that formation (*saṇkhāro*) is impermanent, conditioned, dependently arisen; that craving is impermanent, conditioned, dependently arisen... that feeling, that contact, that ignorance... When one knows and sees thus the immediate destruction of the taints occurs."

This piece works through *paṭicca samuppāda* in reverse order: craving, back to feeling, to contact, and then leaping back to ignorance. Presumably the links between are "assumed" and not needed in order to make the point. But the *saṅkhārā*, coming as they do after craving (so it's *saṅkhārā*, craving, feeling, contact, ignorance) are the sense of self forming; they take shape because they have been fed the experience they need to confirm the theory that self exists.

Ignorance (*avijjā*)

> "And what is ignorance? Not knowing about suffering (*dukkha*), not knowing about the origin of suffering, not knowing about the cessation of suffering, not knowing about the way leading to the cessation of suffering—this is called ignorance. With the arising of the taints there is the arising of ignorance."[64]

Sāriputta's definition of ignorance is easy enough to understand: the problem is that we are ignorant of what exactly *dukkha* is, and what causes it, and so of course we can't know that it can end, or how to end it. On the surface this seems to bear little relation to all that follows, but it is, again, the field, the fodder for the first source of our problems, and it can also be seen as telling us what will follow, because dependent arising is the cure for ignorance. It is the cure because it defines *dukkha*, it shows us its origin, enables us to see that *dukkha* can be ended, and shows us the way to end it.

64 MN 9.66 [pts M i 54]

In the portion of the *sutta* that immediately follows this, the final section, Sāriputta defines the taints, because he has (above) said that the taints are the cause of ignorance.

> "There are these three taints: the taint of sensual desire (*kāmāsavo*), the taint of being (*bhavāsavo*), and the taint of ignorance (*avijjāsavo*)." [65]

We encountered two out of three of these back at *taṇhā*'s craving, where it was *kāmataṇhā*, *bhavataṇhā*, and *vibhavataṇhā* that were being discussed. These lists always seem to start with *kāma*[66], perhaps because even when people hold no strong views about what makes us who we are, or who we will be after death, they still have strong views about things that come to us through our senses: we need this, and don't want that, need even more of this, feel we need a monopoly in it, will go to war over ensuring we have enough of it, whatever it is. All this starts with the senses, as is made clear by the number of times our senses are referred to in the detailed "ritual" portion of dependent arising.

Bhava is about becoming whatever we conceive ourselves to be—in *taṇhā* it was about craving for becoming, which is another way of saying *saṅkhāra*, craving for existence. The forms that this craving for and clinging to existence takes may come in a variety of flavors (*bhava* or *vibhava*; *diṭṭhi* or *sīlabbata* or *attavāda*) but they all seem to revolve around that simple desire to be whatever it is we think we are or should be, and to look for confirmation in the world around us.

If the taints that are the field in which ignorance grows are simply the ways we act, just naturally, in response to our senses (*kāmāsavo*), and our unquestioned desire to prove ourselves to be who we think we are (*bhavāsavo*), perhaps the third taint (*avijjāsavo*) is named ignorance because that's what the other two are, also: all three are how people behave when they don't know any better. Ignorance really needs no first cause: it is just the way we arrive in the world.

Conclusions

With the groundwork laid by Joanna Jurewicz in her 2000 article "Playing With Fire" it became clear that many of the terms in *paṭicca samup-*

[65] MN 9.70 [pts M i 55]

[66] At *upādāna* it was *kāmupādānaṃ*, *diṭṭhupadanaṃ*, *sīlabbatupādānaṃ*, and *attavādupādānaṃ*. In *bhava* it was *kāmabhavo*, *rūpabhavo*, *arūpabhavo*.

pāda made reference to Vedic mythology, and in particular to creation myths about Prajāpati.

Linking those terms to the structure of the great fire ritual, the Agnicayana, in which Prajāpati's creation myth is the metaphor for the creation, perfection, and transformation of the *ātman*, reveals ritual as the structure that is likely to have originally supported the teaching of dependent arising, a structure that was so obvious in its time that it went without overt mention—leaving later generations puzzled.

The confusion of interpretations offered in the past is easily understood through looking at the many layers of meaning incorporated into each link in the chain of events being described.

The overall structure first draws on the model of the conception of the first man from his desire for existence, and the completion of this process in the individuality of name-and-form; next come the details of a life of rituals—the things done over and over again throughout one life; and finally there is a fairly literal description of conception, birth, aging, and death. That structure is modelled on the way a life was viewed in those days: there was the birth out of the mother's womb (first birth), but that didn't really make one a man; there was an initiation ceremony which was seen as the more important "second birth" that gave the upper classes their name of "Twice Born"; and finally, at death, there was the last big ritual which completed the cycle, giving *ātman* the birth that really counted, into a life beyond death (third birth). This Vedic system had the Sacrificer born three times in one life cycle—so it is no wonder that later thinkers, having lost the original context, caught echoes of those three lives and felt that what was being described was the previous life, the present life, and the next life.

On the other hand, the actual model really described only one life—from conception to death and the transition to life beyond death—so those who felt that *paṭicca samuppāda* described one life were right too.

The third popular interpretation of dependent arising has been that it describes the moment by moment appearance and fading of the sense of self. With the very detailed description of how sense information comes to us, is experienced, reacted to, and built upon, which description is followed by birth, aging, and death, this is quite understandable. Because aging and death are equated in the *sutta*s with *dukkha*, it made sense to see what was being described as a birth of that sense of self which results in its suffering, dying, and going around again. Suttas that talk about the rapid arising and passing away of consciousness would seem to support that view too. Unfortunately that view would appear to mean that each moment's arising of that sense of self results in a rapid response of *dukkha*, resulting in the death of that sense of self before the whole thing starts again; but in the *suttas* the fruits of our actions are not described as consistently arriving so fast, so there was clearly something wrong with that model.

What had been missing is the recollection of how, in the days in which the Buddha lived, individuals participated throughout their lives in rituals which were believed to modify their *ātman*—correct problems, bring into being as yet untapped resources, and so on. The process might be seen as similar to building, all throughout a life, a retirement home in some beautiful, distant setting. You go there and work on it a little more each time, perhaps taking out something that didn't work so well, adding some new feature, and when the time comes, it will be perfect and you'll spend the rest of your days there. The *ātman* was not destroyed with each ritual, but was transformed, and arose better than before.

The Buddha preached against such rituals, in part because of the waste of lives of the animals slaughtered in some, like the Agnicayana, and he, along with the Jains, who were also against the sacrifices, seem to have had an effect, because it was not long before the sorts of rituals that were the model, here described as underlying dependent arising, were largely eliminated from brahminical culture. It may well be that the Buddha's use of ritual in dependent arising also played a part, by ridiculing the basis for those rituals, in making them unpopular. What an irony, then, that the strength of his argument eventually made its framework so obscure that the teaching it carried became confused by the terms and the relationships between the pieces.

Seeing the complexity of the structures underlying *paṭicca samuppāda* in this new way not only makes sense, but also makes sense of the ways it was interpreted in the past.

Buddhists have long known that their original teacher denied the existence of the *ātman*, so it comes as no surprise that this interpretation shows him using the popular model of *ātman*'s creation through a life-long series of rituals as the model of how our life-long rituals (aka "habits") lead us to create that which can be mistaken for *ātman*, that aggregate of senses of self. This alternative view of dependent arising's structure reveals a lesson that is entirely consistent with what is said throughout the *suttas*: that there is no eternal self that moves on after death, and that it is the way we react to sensory information that is the key to seeing what it is we are mistaking for that eternal self. This new interpretation of the teaching brings into sharp focus the way in which we invest a bit of ourselves in our definitions of everything we encounter; how we seek and find in the world around us confirmation of our sense of who we are. We do so because we believe that confirmation to be there, and therefore put ourselves into everything, just as Prajāpati did.

CITATION NOTES:

All citations for the Pali *suttas* are given first with reference to Wisdom Publications volumes, when available, followed by their location in the Pali Text Society editions, as follows:

- pts = Pali Text Society
- a letter designation for the volume:
  - M (Majjhima Nikāya)
  - D (Dīgha Nikāya)
  - S (Saṃyutta Nikāya)
  - A (Aṅguttara Nikāya)
  - Sn (Sutta Nipāta)
  - I (Ituvatakka)
  - U (Udāna)
- a roman numeral for the book within the volume
- an Arabic numeral for the PTS page number in that book

A Secular Understanding of Dependent Arising

Chapter 2: A Secular Understanding of Dependent Arising

Introduction

Americans seem to use "dependent origination" as the most common translation of *paticca samuppada*, but I don't think we're talking about "origination" so much as about what is constantly arising, so I prefer "dependent arising". (For the sake of search engines, I used "dependent origination" in the title of each blogpost, but a rose by any other name is still useful to learn about, right?)

The Buddha says of the ignorance that begins this lesson, that it has no discoverable beginning. I take this to mean that in his view, it may have had an origin but it's not one he could see from his perspective. (AN 10.61:)

> "A first beginning of ignorance cannot be conceived, (of which it can be said), 'Before that, there was no ignorance and it came to be after that.' Though this is so, monks, yet a specific condition of ignorance can be conceived. Ignorance, too, has its nutriment, I declare; and it is not without a nutriment."—Translation by Nyanaponika Thera[67]

Nowadays science offers us some reasonable explanations of where the process began, which would have been in improvements in survival mechanisms over aeons. What arises in the process of dependent arising is a mechanism that has served our species well over the course of its evolution: the instinct to see ourselves as distinct and valuable individuals whose lives are worthy of preservation. This system has worked well in creating a creature who will defend itself and its ideas—for both

[67] `http://www.accesstoinsight.org/lib/authors/nyanaponika/wheel238.html#fnt-10-58`

of these (our bodies and our inventions) are key to the success of humankind. But it's quite common for the things that serve us well to also have a dark side, and there is this about our tendency to self-protection: we perhaps take it a little too far. It seems that the instinct that served us well in our primitive days may not serve as well when applied to the increasing complexities of human interactions.

This series of posts is a *secular* understanding of dependent arising in the sense that it describes what's going on in each link in terms of things we can see for ourselves—it is secular because it is confined to the here and now, the mundane, the pragmatic. The focus remains on what is happening in this life, and no reference is made to karma or rebirth.

A quick glance at the terms used for each link of dependent arising make it apparent that the Buddha was talking about a birth that follows a life described in terms of our actions (starting with contact with the world and what we feel in response to that contact). Until fairly recently, it has been assumed that because the links were named with reference to rebirth, the only logical explanation was that what was being discussed was the fact of rebirth—and that *paticca samuppada* was effectively an endorsement of the Buddha's belief in rebirth as the cosmic moral order. However, a new way of looking at the teaching recognizes that the Buddha used the structure of common concepts of the day about rebirth, to deny that what people thought was happening actually was, and to simultaneously point out what he saw was actually going on. This series focuses on the "actually going on" portion; the denial is not covered in these posts, but can be found in a paper called "Burning Yourself" recently published in the Journal of the Oxford Center for Buddhist Studies.

#1 Ignorance

This post is the first in a series of twelve on dependent arising (the translation of *paticca samuppada* that I prefer over dependent origination, or co-dependent arising, or interdependent origination or any of the other variations). I plan to take each link in the classic chain of twelve and explain—in the plainest language I can—what it means to us here and now in our practice.

As some of you may know, dependent arising has been my pet project for about half a decade, now, and I have developed a hypothesis about its structure that I am reasonably sure is correct, not only because

it makes sense in the context of our times, but because it is consistent with what the Buddha taught all through the canon, and, in fact, makes much of what has been obscure make sense. But I'm not going to talk about any of that. If you want to know about the supporting structure, I hope you'll subscribe to the Journal of the Oxford Centre for Buddhist Studies[68]—a new, wide-ranging, open-minded publication that was started recently by Professor Richard Gombrich—and get your very own copy of the paper "Burning Yourself". Understanding the context provided by the paper should make a big difference to sutta-readers' insights into what's being said all throughout the canon, since dependent arising is the big lesson that ties the teachings on the dharma together. Subscribing will also have the effect of supporting Prof. Gombrich's work, which opens up Buddhism to wider discussion than in the past, so a subscription is a doubly-good "safe bet".

I'm going to start each post with Sariputta's run-down of what the link in the chain is about, and I'll often make reference to the step before, and the one that follows, but I am going to try to keep it simple and practical. The sutta I will use is MN 9 (pts M i 46-55 as translated by Bhikkhus Nanamoli and Bodhi). It is Sariputta's answer to the question "What is right view?" To summarize, he says that right view is understanding what is wholesome (and unwholesome), understanding nutriment, and the four noble truths, and each of twelve steps of dependent origination, and the taints. The talk about wholesomeness is not difficult to understand (it is general morality); nutriment we have covered in previous posts[69]; and the four noble truths should be familiar to just about everyone (if not, they are the focus of the last half

[68] `http://www.ocbs.org/journal`

[69] `http://secularbuddhism.org/2012/01/31/nutriment/` and `http://secularbuddhism.org/2012/02/18/food-and-fire-in-dependent-origination/`

of this post). We can talk about the taints at the end of the series if anyone is still with me at that point.

Before we start on the first link, I will finally add my answer to the earlier Pop Quiz[70] about Dependent Origination and just say this about what dependent arising is: it describes the arising of the parts of our sense-of-self that cause problems. Using Pali terms, I would say it describes how *anatta* arises, causing *dukkha*.

Regarding my use (and abuse) of the term "*anatta*", there are some Pali terms I use in preference to any English translation. Among these are *dukkha* and *sankhara*—covered in the next post—terms I find necessary to use because there is no good corresponding word for them in English. *Anatta* I am loosely translating as "sense-of-self" though it's more specific than that. The Buddha didn't overtly use the term *anatta* the way I use it—he seems to have meant it to be read, primarily, as a denial that there is a lasting self (that's what *anatta* means—not-self) and was very careful not to give it any sense of concreteness. However, the overall "shape" of dependent arising indicates to me that describing the end product of the process as "*anatta*" in our time is not in conflict with what the Buddha was trying to convey. Therefore, I break with both the original use, and with convention by using it as a label for a concept that can be generally described as "that which we mistake for a lasting self" (but it is still more complex than even that).

Dependent arising also, in a way, describes impermanence, because at the base of it all, the Buddha is really showing us what happens so that we can see both that what arises is impermanent, and how to keep it from happening in the first place (therefore proving its impermanence when we put a stop to it). But the main thing it is describing is just our fluid sense-of-self, its origin, and by extension, how we can end the process. The reason it details all this is because the end-product of that sense of self is *dukkha*. So we could say that *paticca samuppada* describes all three of "the three marks of existence": not-self (*anatta*), *dukkha* (aka "suffering"), and impermanence (*anicca*).

One important key to keep in mind when considering dependent arising is that each link in the chain represents something active, rather than static. A possible exception would be ignorance, depending on how you look at it. All of these describe things going on in a process.

---

[70] http://secularbuddhism.org/2011/08/02/pop-quiz-what-is-dependent-arising/

The first step in the link is ignorance, and here is Sariputta's description of it:

> Not knowing about suffering, not knowing about the origin of suffering, not knowing about the cessation of suffering, not knowing about the way leading to the cessation of suffering—this is called ignorance. With the arising of the taints there is the arising of ignorance. With the cessation of the taints there is the cessation of ignorance.

Basically, the ignorance we're talking about is ignorance of what is meant by *dukkha* (suffering). It is not ignorance that there is *dukkha*—we all experience it—and not ignorance of there being a term for it, but more like a misidentification of what it is/what the problem is. The question then gets framed in terms of "the four noble truths": What is *dukkha*, where does it come from, can it be stopped, and how would that work?

Translated into plain English—and given that what's being described is the arising of our sense-of-self—what we are ignorant of is:

(1) That it is that "sense of self" (*anatta*) that causes the problem of *dukkha*—and by extension, it is only problems generated by that sense of self that are the definition of *dukkha*. This means that *dukkha* is not physical pain, or our own death, or aging, or sadness for the problems of the world, or even the keen pain we may feel at the loss of a loved-one—unless we have added unnecessary layers onto those things, grounded in a sense of self: the "why me"s and "I'll never survive without you" and "it was all my fault" or even blaming others for what we feel.

(2) We are ignorant not only of what that *dukkha* is, but where it is coming from—which is from that sense-of-self, and from our own ignorance about that sense of self.

(3) We are not only unaware that *dukkha* has its source in the sense of self, but that something can be done about it. As long as we remain unaware of what's happening, we have no power to fix it.

(4) Once we become aware of all of the above, we can end our ignorance of the process by learning to see it through the tools provided in dependent arising, and the path of practice the Buddha laid out.

The four items listed above are the four noble truths reworded to show that dependent arising is the answer to the questions those truths pose. It is actually "the cure" for *dukkha*; it is one of the tools. It tells us what *dukkha* is, how it originates, and shows us that the process can be interrupted, and gives us the structured insights that allow us to do that. Ignorance, then, is "the first cause" of our problems and understanding that is the first step in the cure for ignorance.

#2 Sankhara

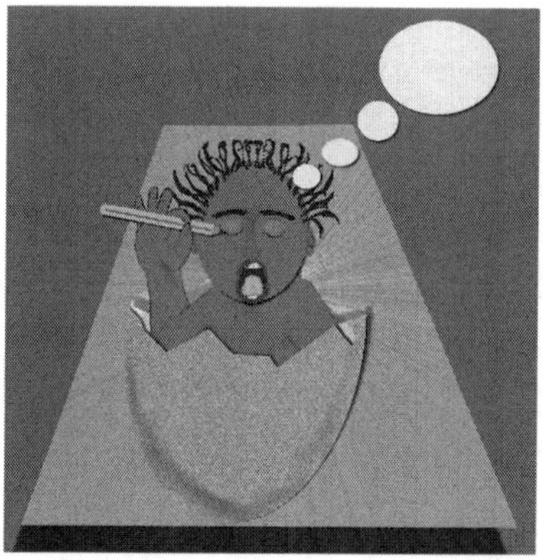

In the last post I offered a fairly plain description of what was meant by "ignorance" in the first link in the chain of dependent arising. It is ignorance of what *dukkha* is, how it comes about, that it can come to an end, and the way to do that. I said that *dukkha* is caused by a particular sense-of-self (the sense that we have a lasting self), and that it is never the sort of suffering that is completely out of our control, but is defined by being something we do have control over, it is the extra bit of drama we tend to add to events, drama centered on us, "my problem, my fault, my pain"—never just "pain, problem, no fault".

Because what dependent arising describes is how *dukkha* comes about —through the development of our sense of self (and it describes that, too)—this one teaching is the answer to our ignorance.

Understanding dependent arising gives us the tool we need to break the cycles.

The second step is called "*sankhara*" and is not as easy to explain—it has always given teachers and translators problems—but let's see how it goes this time.

We'll start with Sariputta's description in MN 9, as translated by Bhikkhus Nanamoli and Bodhi, who translate *sankhara* as "formations":

> There are these three kinds of formations: the bodily formation, the verbal formation, the mental formation. With the arising of ignorance there is the arising of formations. With the cessation of ignorance there is the cessation of formations.

This tells us *sankhara* has something to do with body (actions), speech, and thoughts, but doesn't tell us a whole lot more than that. The reason for this is because Sariputta's talk focuses on "the nutriment" for each step. He is specifically pointing out the "field" that is going to grow what goes on here, and so he's telling us to look at what we do to see what's happening: watch our bodily activities, our speech, and our thoughts.

When looking at a field to spot what arises in it that is part of a problem, we need to remember that lots of things tend to grow up in the same field, and not all of them are going to be the problem. Let's work a moment with this metaphor: We have a field we want to plant with good things that will sustain a good life, but it has been left to grow wild on its own. There may be some things in the field that grew naturally that are good and useful and will feed us while we work in the field, but most of what grows there without a care from us are weeds. As we learn how to be a successful custodian of the field, we learn what things grow in the field that need to be pulled up (the weeds), what healthy things to encourage (what's already there that we should water and care for) and as the weeds disappear, we can plant useful seeds in the spaces left behind—and having them grow there will help keep the weeds out. This is, effectively, a metaphor for Buddhist practice. At each step we are replacing the weeds that grow just naturally on their own, with something more useful.

The important thing to realize is that not everything that grows in a field is a weed.

To take this concept out of the metaphor, what I'm saying is that not every action in body, speech, and mind is a problem. The problem is specifically the things we do and say and think that have as one of their primary causes the ignorance we covered in the last post (the ignorance is the lack of care that lets the weed seeds take root). The narrowing of the definition of what we're talking about in each step—so that we have to pay attention to which item in the field is the one that's the problem—is inherent in the nature of a chain of causal events: every later event is colored by the earlier conditions (see Note on causal chains below for an example that may make this clearer). Everything that arises in the entire rest of the cycle has to be able to be labeled "due to ignorance" (of *dukkha*, its cause, cessation, method to end—always due to that specific ignorance).

In this sutta, translating *sankhara* as "activities" would be almost adequate, but "activities" is not all that it describes—the word is touching on something much larger, which I'll try to describe.

Since Sariputta doesn't tell us what to look for in those fields, since he's not specifying what is being nourished with those activities, I'll see if I can describe it: it's part of our natural desire to continue to exist; it's all the unnecessary things we do to shore up our sense of self, and to shape it, and to keep it safe in a world where everyone out there seems to want to change us and shape us to their needs. *Sankhara* describes both the things we do to preserve our sense of self (the activities) and the drive to keep doing that. It describes the hunger to know who we are in relation to the world, to know that we exist, and to protect what we do know about ourselves, and the knowledge of our existence. It is both the drive and the actions that spring from that drive.

So when Sariputta suggests that what nourishes *sankhara* is our mental, physical, and verbal activities, he is advising us to look at what we do, say, and think, that brings about our sense of self—look at our activities to see in action our drive to do this; look for the ways we do this. Look, too, for the ways in which the things we do feed the drive even more—for example, how that sense of satisfaction we get when we confirm our opinions about something make us want more of that feeling.

But wait! There's more! For the same low-low price of one word—*sankhara*—we're going to throw in one more meaning as a bonus! Because one of the most important things to understand about *sankhara* is that it is not describing evil deeds—it is from this sense of *sankhara* that Buddhism draws its "no sin" approach to life. The things that we do that are driven by *sankhara*, that are *sankharas* when they occur, may indeed be seen as evil, some may even be intentionally evil—but *sankhara*'s cause, you may recall, is not evil, it is ignorance.

The problem with *sankhara* is that we don't even know we have this drive and we certainly don't know how it plays out—at least not at the start. And even when we do learn about it, there are still going to be hundreds of ways it gets us into trouble without us having spotted individual tactics it uses for our self-preservation. There is a lot of ignorance to learn about, to look for, to spot, and it isn't easy to break the habits that have formed around many of these underlying, unexamined assumptions about how the world works and what our part in it is or should be. Even when we identify the activities, it can be a challenge to put a stop to them.

But the point I'm making here is that *sankhara* is, primarily, our nature, it is our underlying tendencies. What it really is, is the survival mechanism that has gotten us where we are as a species—a survival mechanism run amok. Our need to feel that we are alive and that we are worth keeping alive, and to protect ourselves, is necessary (therefore it is not *sankhara*, and activities supporting the basics aren't *sankhara*-activities), but our somewhat obsessive need to protect every damned thing about us is unnecessary, and it is the source of most of our problems. The basic need to take care of ourselves (seeking food, water, shelter, medicines) have nothing to do with *sankhara*; those are the things that grow in the same field, but they aren't the ones we're after. It's when we get into the complexities of human interactions that self-preservation sometimes gets in the way. It's an old, reptile-brain system that can't keep up with the times.

Did you think I was done packing value into this one word? I'm not! There is actually one more layer to *sankhara*, and that is that it is supported by the nature of the society we live in—by its customs and assumptions. It is not just created by our natural tendencies. The word "*sankhara*" as a Buddhist term derives from a word for rituals, specifically rituals used in community with others. We come into the world with an overactive need to develop certainty about ourselves and the way the world works, and the things we are told by our parents, friends, teachers, and everyone we encounter contribute to the ways in which we develop that certainty. Our natural tendency to develop views about the self gets directed along lines supported by society, and our tendencies feed off of society's assumptions. If everyone around us seems to be saying that the path to happiness lies in being beautiful, or acquiring wealth or power—or worshipping God in a certain way—we will tend to head in that direction, too.

Sankhara and its primary cause, ignorance, in their place at the beginning of dependent arising, are part of an early sequence that, really, describes our nature. The Buddha was telling us that we come into the world in this state: ignorant, with a strong desire for existence, and the ability to do what it takes to protect our sense of self. We aren't even aware we are like that, and that's where the trouble begins.

NOTE on causal chains: In any causal chain the field of possible items we are looking at is narrowed by each event—by all events—that came before. If we are looking at an end product of a sick patient who has celiac disease (CD), we would start by considering the genetic makeup of the parents. One or the other of the parents carries the gene for CD.

The two conceive a child—the child conceived is not just any child, it is a child of the type who has one or more parents who carried the CD gene—this is true of the patient at the end of the chain, just as it is true of the patient at the beginning of the chain: the field "children" has been narrowed to a smaller group. In the next step in the causal chain we say that the patient is one who inherited that gene from one of the parents. We are now talking about a patient who had a parent with the CD gene, and who inherited it. We are NOT talking about a patient whose parents had the gene who did NOT inherit it—the field just got narrower (from all people who had at least one parent with the gene, to the same field but now leaving out those who didn't inherit it). In the next link in the chain, there needs to be exposure to gluten. We are now talking about a patient who had a parent with the gene (not one whose parents didn't); who inherited the gene (not one who didn't inherit it); who has been exposed to gluten (not one who got the gene but has no exposure to gluten). The field of potential candidates gets narrower with each step. At the next step we have someone who has a triggering event that activates the gene—not someone who has all the previous conditions but NEVER has a triggering event. At the next step we have someone who remains exposed to gluten, not someone who removes gluten from their diet—until by the end we have something very specific being described, having met all the conditions that came before. By the end of the chain what we are talking about has a much smaller set of possible candidates than the pool we drew from in the first step, but the condition of the first step (people who have one parent with the gene) is still just as crucial a factor at the end as it was at the beginning.

#3 Consciousness

We come into the world ignorant of the things we do that end up causing *dukkha* in our lives, and in particular ignorant of the drive for existence of our sense-of-self: that's step #1: ignorance, and step #2: *sankhara*. *Sankhara* is simultaneously that natural tendency to develop and protect our sense-of-self taken to extremes, and *sankharas* are the things we do that create and develop that identity. *Sankhara*, in that dual sense, represents the whole chain of dependent arising: it is the drive and the actions (including our thoughts); everything else is just details.

The third link in the chain addresses the beginning point of the *sankhara* process. It is usually translated as consciousness, which is a fair enough translation of its Pali term, "vinnana". But given that it is a very specific kind of consciousness, I actually prefer the term "awareness" as being less confusing when describing what it does.

Here's Sariputta's explanation of vinnana, from MN 9, as translated by Bhikkhus Nanamoli and Bodhi

> There are these six classes of consciousness: eye-consciousness, ear-consciousness, nose-consciousness, tongue-consciousness, body-consciousness, mind-consciousness. This is called consciousness.

We are back in "a field" again, which serves to nourish the events in the cycle being described, but pointing out the field doesn't give us detail about what's actually going on in that consciousness that's the issue. It is not every activation of "eye-consciousness" (for example) that is part of the problem, only *sankhara*-driven instances are.

What is made clear with this list is that this "consciousness" is something that comes in through the senses, and elsewhere we find the Buddha describing that this is something that arises with incoming data, develops, then passes away. This is why I prefer "awareness" as a translation, because we are talking about something that exists only when there is sense data to take note of. We may feel something—say a rumble of hunger in the belly—and then, even as awareness of the feeling fades, we think about it, and as we tell ourselves stories about the hunger, we may go on to thinking about what we should eat though the feeling that triggered the line of thought has long since vanished. Soon some other sensation will replace the hunger, and we'll be off on another series of thoughts.

Note that describing the process as one that comes, grows, and fades has consciousness/awareness in the role of something that only exists while it is being fed—this is the very epitome of the concept of nourishment and existence that prevailed in the Buddha's day. The potential for awareness is always there, but it isn't active (it isn't "real") until it is being fed, until it finds what it is looking for.

But we need to remember that this awareness is of a very specific type. As with *sankhara*, when we look at the field of sense-awareness, not every event that arises is the awareness we're talking about, but only the sort of sense-awareness that is grounded in *sankhara*, which is the driving force for this kind of awareness. This is awareness that is seeking whatever is out there that will best serve the needs of its own existence—the drive to protect our self, to know how everything in the world relates to us, to find advantage in it and be wary of disadvantage. Again, we are *not* talking about the most basic survival needs—how to get food, water, shelter—these things in their simplest forms are not the problem; they are not the problem because they are not the things we do that result in *dukkha*; they are not the problem because they don't have as their source the beyond-necessity drives of *sankhara*. It's when desires around preserving self get taken to extremes that they are *sankhara*-awareness. For example, the need for power can be seen as wanting to make sure one will always have enough of the basics to never be threatened with having too little, and therefore accumulating goods beyond bare necessities—which results, whether we realize it or not, in a disadvantage to others.

One thing the Buddha emphasizes about this kind of awareness is that it is interdependent with the next step—these are the only two steps described as being interdependent (that is, with each one being a cause of the other)—and it is because the very definition of awareness is of something that does not exist unless it is fed that it is bound up with the next step, because the next step is its food, as we will see in the next post.

#4 Name-and-Form

It is with this link in the chain that this secular understanding of dependent arising finds a deeper insight into the processes through which we create *anatta*, deeper insight than offered by the confusion of the traditional views of what's going on. The Pali word for this step is *nama-rupa*—*nama* shares a root with our "name" and *rupa* means "form". My preferred term for these—not in translations but in explanations of what they're about—is "identification".

But let's let Sariputta have his say (from MN 9, as translated by Thanissaro Bhikkhu[71]):

[71] `http://www.accesstoinsight.org/tipitaka/mn/mn.009.than.html`

> "Feeling, perception, intention, contact, & attention: This is called name. The four great elements, and the form dependent on the four great elements: This is called form. This name & this form are called name-&-form."

At first glance, this explanation of Sariputta's seems to have broken the pattern—it seems to be describing what each part of name-and-form is, rather than describing the field *namarupa*'s activities grow in, but that's not what's going on here; it is still the field.

What *namarupa* is, is the way we identify things, and the way we identify with them. We use feeling, perception, intention, contact, and the direction of our attention to sort out what's what; we also use the shape of things, their physical, material forms. These habits of thought are the fields in which we grow the things we do that are *sankhara*-based.

The previous step's "awareness" is a primary cause of the events in this step, because it is our *sankhara*-driven awareness that is behind our drive to sort everything in the world in a way that relates to us—this is why I say it's about identification: we identify what we encounter—recognize its form, give it a name—and then we identify with it, sorting into (in the Buddha's terms) "pleasant, unpleasant, or neither of these" or (in my terms) of advantage to us, or disadvantage, or "makes no difference". We define everything by how it relates to us. It is simply our nature to do this—we do it without being aware that we are doing it (out of ignorance).

Awareness—driven by our need to exist (*sankhara*), to protect ourselves, to know ourselves in relation to the world—is, itself, the driving force for the way we use our abilities and our senses to identify whatever we encounter (be it objects or experiences or ideas) in terms of whether it supports our ideas about ourselves, or denies them, whether it will help us, or hinder us.

But awareness doesn't exist without something to feed on, and it feeds on the way we identify the world in relation to our selves. Sense data comes in and we identify with it in some way, and because we do this, awareness can keep on seeking. Having found confirmation of itself, having been fed, it goes on looking for more, more, more, always needing to be fed. So, for example, our hungry awareness encounters an idea—it turns the idea over, examining its form, its qualities, and compares it to itself. Is this idea "like me"? Or is it very different from me? If it fits in my concept of myself, I am drawn to it; if it is too strange, too different from my own ideas, I am averse to it. If it seems to have no value at all, it gets ignored.

Again, this is just what we do by nature, no blame, no sin, just the default behavior we all share.

The desire to exist drives awareness to seek confirmation that we exist (and looks for detail about who we are) through the way we identify with the world—awareness drives identification—and confirmation that we exist through identification with the world drives awareness to keep seeking. The two are mutually dependent.

#5 Use of the Six Senses

When Sariputta describes step #5 (from MN 9, as translated by Bhikkhus Nanamoli and Bodhi), we are clearly in the field:

> There are these six bases: the eye-base, the ear-base, the nose-base, the tongue-base, the body-base, the mind-base...

This tells us nothing about how it relates to the process of dependent origination, it only tells us where to look—in what field this step will grow. We can be certain that we are looking at the senses, but what exactly are we looking for? With my amazing supernormal powers I can see that "contact" is coming up next, so this isn't talking about the senses in the process of being fed by their particular objects, instead it is still-hungry senses. Driven by our innate desire to figure out who we are and how we relate to the world—what's for us, and what's against us—to categorize and classify everything in terms of our self, and to shore up our already developed sense of self with more and more data, this is our senses reaching out to look for that information.

If you've ever been lucky enough to sit in meditation and manage to get settled enough to have discursive thought go quiet, reaching one of those wonderful moments of peace and equanimity, you might also have encountered the arising of a little bubble of pressure in your mind, as if a thought is trying to take form, but formless still, so you have no idea what it will be. In the silence of the moment, your senses may be

reaching for something to feed awareness, because it's hungry and not being fed images of itself. That would describe this step in action: the senses—driven by awareness and the need to find evidence that can be sorted into categories that prove we are who we think we are—are trying to find something to settle on to satisfy that drive.

These first five steps have been describing the situation as it is given to us by nature. These are the initial conditions that are there as an underlying tendency from the very first, but that don't develop into anything active until a little later in life. The Buddha talks about this underlying tendency when he describes the reason why an infant isn't a liberated being:

> For a young tender infant lying prone does not even have the notion 'identity,' so how could identity view arise in him? Yet the underlying tendency to identity view lies within him.—MN 64 Bhikkhus Nanamoli& Bodhi's translation

That underlying tendency doesn't get watered and grow until a bit later in life. In one of the most detailed suttas on dependent arising, MN 38[72], the Buddha describes conception, gestation, birth, infancy and toddlerhood, through a childhood of playing with toys. It is just at this point that the awareness of the senses are introduced, and shortly after that:

> ...he is infatuated with pleasing forms, and gets upset over unpleasing forms ... he relishes any feeling he feels— pleasure, pain, neither-pleasure-nor-pain—welcomes it, & remains fastened to it. As he relishes that feeling, welcomes it, & remains fastened to it, delight arises. Now, any delight in feeling is clinging/sustenance. From his clinging/sustenance as a requisite condition comes becoming. From becoming as a requisite condition comes birth. From birth as

[72] Translation by Thanissaro Bhikkhu, `http://www.accesstoinsight.org/tipitaka/mn/mn.038.than.html`

> a requisite condition, then aging-&-death, sorrow, lamentation, pain, distress, and despair come into play. Such is the origination of this entire mass of stress & suffering.

So it is somewhere past the point in life when one is doing somersaults and playing with sticks that the underlying tendency to "identity view" (the problematic sense that we have a lasting self), nourished by the way we like and dislike what we experience, becomes food ("sustenance") for the birth of something. The next section of links describes the events that start taking place at that point in life, that act to feed that growing sense of self.

We end this overview section with a link in the chain of dependent arising that tells us that all that came before is now driving the senses to look for confirmation-of-self, and with the next step we'll find the senses having succeeded—that is the essence of "contact"—it is a specific instance of contact between the senses and the world that satisfies all the conditions that came before it.

#6 Contact

Up to this point what has been covered in the first five steps is an overview of the problematic situation as it's given to us. The model for what's going on in these first five steps is a well-known origin myth that gets referred to in various different places in the suttas: the story of the first man, Prajapati (whose role got taken over by Brahma). In using the structure of the story of Prajapati's creation—and the creation of all of us—the Buddha was clearly describing the parallel story of what he sees as important about the way we come to be as we are, as well, only the details of his story are a *little* different than the original. (For details on the story of Prajapati and how it can be seen to be part of the structure of dependent arising, please see the paper "Burning Yourself".)

The first five steps tell us that we come into the world ignorant (#1) of what's about to be described, and what's described is a process that results in *dukkha*. It begins with a drive for the existence of a lasting self, and for knowledge of that self (that drive is *sankhara* #2) which is activated—satisfied, fed, and made real—when our ever-hungry consciousness (#3) becomes aware of something that feeds it what it is seeking. What feeds it is a particular piece of information that comes in through the senses, that we can perceive as confirming that we are who we think we are and that the world behaves as we

think it does (that's "name-and-form" #4 aka "identification"). This sequence of five steps, closely following the myth, ends up with the senses being directed (#5) to look for the information that *sankhara* drives us to seek. With the sixth step, "contact" we leave the overview that describes the "givens" of our life and enter the realm of a detailed description of how the process plays out.

With Sariputta's description we are, again, back in the field of the senses, in this case with any one of them making contact with its object. Because this is the first link in the chain that describes an actual sequence of events, this is the earliest point at which we can notice the process that is dependent arising taking place.

> There are these six classes of contact: eye-contact, ear-contact, nose-contact, tongue-contact, body-contact, mind-contact. With the arising of the sixfold base there is the arising of contact.—MN 9 translated by Bhikkhus Nanamoli and Bodhi

One of the questions that has often been asked about dependent arising's chain of events, when offered as a description of a process that needs to be stopped, is "What does it mean to stop contact?" as well as "Why would I want to stop consciousness?" If the descriptions given thusfar are mistaken for literal descriptions of what's going on (a reasonable assumption to make, given that this is the way we describe things in our times) rather than recognized as the field things grow in, then ending consciousness and contact would mean literally ceasing to experience the world—flatlining, in the case of consciousness. Not a good thing. But the reason these questions always come up is because we have misunderstood the descriptions: they are not what is happening but where it is happening.

The other clue that is often missed is that each link not only depends on the previous link, but all the previous links. By the time we get to "contact" we have very narrowly defined it as contact that is grounded in ignorance of *dukkha*. It is contact that is specifically created from ignorance of what *dukkha* is and how it happens, that ignorance being important to the contact. It is contact driven by *sankhara*'s desire for existence, as well as by the actions we take as a result of that desire, since, included in those actions are the ways in which our consciousness always seeks information that supports its awareness of itself, and the ways in which we divide the world up in terms of ourselves. The contact comes directly from the senses that have been actively seeking the information that will satisfy *sankhara*, awareness, and our desire to define the world as relating to us.

There may be contacts that don't make reference to any of that. Certainly, in our practices of mindfulness and meditation, there are moments when we may manage to just hear the car with blaring music that booms and vibrates into our bellies as "sounds and vibration" and not as a serious annoyance that is interrupting the quiet moment. When we manage to not be labeling experience in terms of ourselves, not assigning it to categories of pleasant or unpleasant and telling ourselves further stories about it—when we can let go of all that and just be—then we have contact of a different sort. Contact that isn't even asked "are you for me or against me" is not the contact dependent arising is showing us we can end. In the same way, consciousness that is not about seeking the self or advantage is not what we are wanting to stop. In both cases it is a very narrowly defined part of a very specific process that we are seeking to bring to an end.

#7 Feeling

> There are these six classes of feeling: feeling born of eye-contact, feeling born of ear-contact, feeling born of nose-contact, feeling born of tongue-contact, feeling born of body-contact, feeling born of mind-contact.—MN 9 translated by Bhikkhus Nanamoli and Bodhi

Still in the field of sense information, here we are being asked to look at what feelings arise in response to the contact through the senses. It is at the moment of contact and with the rapid arising of feeling in response to that contact that we have our earliest opportunity to stop the whole process.

In other suttas, feeling is described in a way that is more like our modern definitions: as feelings of pleasure, pain, or neither of those. This gives us information about what sorting we are doing that is more useful to us in seeing what is going on than just "feeling that results from contact with a sense". Even so, this is still telling us what to look at, but not how it fits into the process that is being described. We look and see pleasure, or pain, or that we don't care about what our senses just came into contact with—so what?

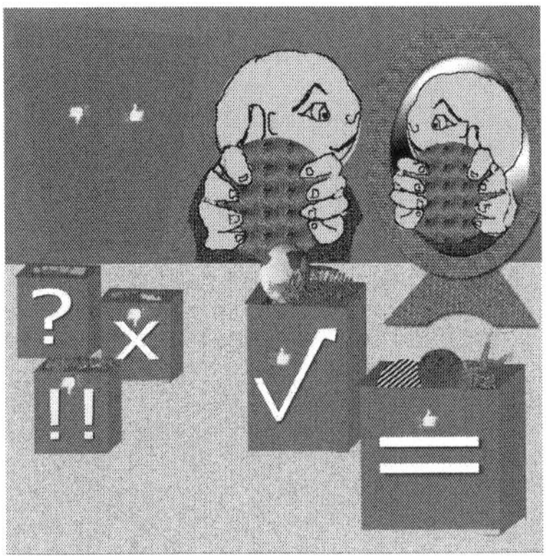

The answer to that question is provided by observing the larger picture—where have we just come from (the effects of *sankhara*'s drives) and where does the process lead? Fortunately this middle portion of the chain of events has been well-interpreted over the years as being the way our encounters with the world lead us into having opinions about things—we'll see why this is clear in the next couple of steps—but it is important to notice that the usual descriptions of each link don't describe what is happening, but what to look at to see what is happening. This is even true of noticing what our experience of contact is: we sort it, but why do we sort it? What is the basis of our categories? That information has been provided by the earlier sections, so it is not what is discussed in the link itself. The driving force comes from the links before this; they plant the seed in this field. Without that seed, what grows in this field will not be whatever produces *dukkha*.

Just as with the previous links, when we look at the field—in this case of feelings—there are things that grow in the field that are not going to bring about *dukkha*, and so are not the problem. Simple hunger and the recognition that we need food is not about an overwrought sense of self—it's just about needing the requisites, and the Buddha allowed the requisites as necessary: food, water, clothes, shelter, medicines, none of these are a hindrance to breaking free of the cycle. It's only when we go over the top with them, and incorporate them into our sense of who we are, and find ourselves needing more or better than others have, that we have problems. So feelings not entwined with a sense of self but just with basic human needs aren't the feelings that end with liberation. By extension, it's possible to recognize that there are feelings that are not a problem; the Buddha names them: compassion, joy in others' accomplishments, friendliness, equanimity. We can see from this that what's being said when we discuss breaking the links in DA and ending all of these is not *all* human feeling (just as it's not all desire for existence, or all awareness, or—looking further along the chain—all aging and all death) but only the parts of these that are involved with the production of *dukkha*.

#8 Craving

> There are these six classes of craving: craving for forms, craving for sounds, craving for odors, craving for flavors, craving for tangibles, craving for mind-objects.—MN 9 translated by Bhikkhus Nanamoli & Bodhi

What is being defined by "craving for sense-objects" is actually far more complex than the simple words of the sutta indicate. This has to be so—it has to be complex—because what's happening here is conditioned by all that has gone before. The simple-sounding field of the senses is provided because everything we are seeking from the beginning has to come to us through our senses (as defined by the Buddha to include the mind and ideas). Whether it's that we want more wine to drown our sorrows, or to hear people agree with our convictions, it all starts with the senses, so that's the field.

But what this is really saying is that when the senses have followed the directions given them by our need to define who we are, how the world relates to us, and to seek confirmation that we're right about our conclusions about who we are and how things serve us, and they have made contact with something that relates to this quest, and feeling has arisen of the good / bad / indifferent variety, we then go on to want more of the same.

It's fairly obvious that we crave the things that shore up our sense of self, and that we feel will be of advantage to us. It's usually stated that aversion may seem like the opposite of craving but it isn't, because it is wanting to get away from something, wanting to move toward comfortable feelings so it is still a sort of craving. But I believe something more is being expressed here, which is that the craving is for confirmation of self, regardless of whether it is about something we are drawn to or averse to. Whether someone says, "You are brilliant!" and we eat up the praise as confirmation that we really are that good, or someone says, "You are so stupid you've totally deluded yourself!" and we suddenly find this person disagreeable, so obviously their opinion doesn't count, it is all about confirming who I am in relation to the world, defining the world in terms of me. So, for example, "That person who disagrees with me is clearly no good / stupid / deluded" defines that person in terms of good/bad for me. It is that confirmation that we crave, more than any individual object or ideology.

This link, then, describes the way, in response to an initial feeling, we react to it by wanting to be fed more of this type of experience: more information that can help develop and sustain a sense of "who I am".

#9 Clinging

> There are these four kinds of clinging: clinging to sensual pleasures, clinging to views, clinging to rituals and observances, and clinging to a doctrine of self.—MN 9 translated by Bhikkhus Nanamoli & Bodhi

The word translated as "clinging" is "upadana" and it actually makes reference to fuel—another form of nutriment, or food—so what we have here is the fuel of views, of rituals and observances, and of belief in the self, as well as the fuel of "sensual pleasures" (though I do not think that what's meant there is limited to sensuality, but is, again, about everything *sankhara*-satisfying that comes in through the senses).

It might seem like this is simply saying, "Clinging to views: bad idea." And regarding certain views (views conditioned by *sankhara*) this is true, just as it is for every other field we've discussed so far (good things also grow in these fields, but we're looking out for the things that derive from *sankhara*). But it's really asking us to watch what grows from the fuel provided by these views, views that support our sense that we have a lasting self, and sometimes even our sense that we know what that self is, and who is similar to us, and who is different. So the view that living in a house is better for our health than living on the streets in a cardboard box isn't a problematic view—it's not based in an excessive sense of self; not all views are a problem, only those driven by the whole chain before, the ones centered on an excessively needy self.

The process of forming opinions starts back with noting feeling as pleasant, unpleasant or neutral, gets further sorted in terms of what we should do with that which is pleasant (get more of it) and with the unpleasant (get less of it) and the neutral (ignore it), until we get here and begin to develop opinions strongly tied into our identity because they are driven by a need to have an identity.

#10 Becoming

> There are these three kinds of being: sense-sphere being, fine-material being and immaterial being.—MN 9 translated by Bhikkhus Nanamoli & Bodhi

This link is second only to *sankhara* in giving translators and students of Buddhism trouble. The examples of the field are not much help to us because they are embedded in their time and place, making reference to things that are no concern of ours now. This is not the same as saying that they are meaningless to us. Two of the three spheres get mentioned in relation to levels of meditation, and it is clear that some of the people of the time felt that when they reached these states they had reached "that other world", so these represent the desired outcome from leading a good life: go to the world where one takes form (and lives happily ever after in bliss), or go to the world where one becomes totally absorbed in Union with the Great All (and forever after experience bliss), or—the third option seems likely as—simply return to the world of the senses (and hopefully enjoy sensual bliss).

The three "spheres" are various conceptions of where the self goes after death: back into the world of the senses, taking form in the world beyond, or being diffused into union with brahman, and though you and I may not have these particular conceptions about what happens to us after we die, each of us has our own variants on these beliefs. We might believe that when we die we are just gone, our constituent parts dissolved and diffused into the matter of our world in its place as part of the universe. Some might believe that when one dies one goes on to heaven (if we are good) and that would be comparable to living happily ever after in bliss in company with the deities of the day. Others may believe that we reincarnate into a new life. It really doesn't matter what form our beliefs take, they still shape our sense of self, and how we behave in the world. Any sense of certainty about what happens after we die is liable to be based on far too little information, and yet we do tend to develop certainty. Even without concerning ourselves with what happens after death (for years I conceived of myself as an open-minded agnostic with no opinion on the subject) we still tend to perceive of ourselves as having a lasting self for the duration of this life at least, and it is our nature to at least hope, at some level, that that self will survive death, or at the very least hope that that self has a meaning that will outlast our short stay here on the planet.

If you object to the above statement, feeling it doesn't apply to you, remember, first, that we are talking about conceptions of self that are founded on ignorance. If you are a practicing Buddhist who has some understanding of what the Buddha taught, you may have less of a tendency to hold beliefs about having a lasting self than many folks do, because you've been paying attention, and learned skills to look for that self—and you've probably not found it. But even so (if you are like me) you may find as you keep probing that there are little pockets of belief you hadn't known were there (it was not until I realized how uncertain my fate after death actually was that I discovered I was not as agnostic as I had thought—I was still holding out hope that I would somehow survive).

What "becoming" is pointing out to us is the ways in which our opinions about who we are get shaped into beliefs about who we are; this is what we should be looking for, because those opinions are the field in which beliefs grow, and the beliefs blossom into something else entirely, as the next step shows us.

#11 Birth

> The birth of beings into the various orders of beings, their coming to birth, precipitation [in a womb][73], generation, manifestation of the aggregates, obtaining the bases for contact—this is called birth. With the arising of being there is the arising of birth.—MN 9, Bhikkhus Nanamoli & Bodhi's translation.

On one level, Sariputta's description of birth is, like the preceding links' details, telling us about the field in which what happens in this step grows: because we are born (because we exist at all) who we are—or at least who we think we are—can become apparent in the world. But the field for this step is actually the birth of our sense of self. In that sense, the "birth" is of an identity/self-concept coming into visible appearance—and what makes our individual self concepts visible in the world is our actions.

Actions, in the Buddha's lessons about what really matters, are in "body, speech, and mind". It may seem a little odd to us to have "mind actions" but it's not only what we do or say, but what we choose not to do or say, as well, that counts. When we choose to refrain from doing or saying something, that "action" takes place only in our minds and so, obviously, is not something we see or hear—but it still makes a difference. Our beliefs about who we are, driven by all the earliest steps, formed through our experiences in the world—good, bad, indifferent—touching on whatever seems like us, unlike us, or neither, developing into certainty, taking shape in our beliefs about ourselves and where

[73] As noted elsewhere (i.e. on my own blog) I have serious doubts about our modern translations of the definition of "birth" in descriptions of dependent arising. The phrase [in a womb] does not appear in the Pali but is, apparently, inserted here by Bhikkhu Bodhi to clarify what he feels is being said, but I suspect there are more problems with the translation than just that. Open-minded students of Pali are invited to have a look at my blog post `http://justalittledust.com/blog/?p=503` and see if they see what I see, at all, and if they can improve on the translation.

we are headed, are given visible form in the world by the things we do that are based on those experiences and beliefs.

Our "being" takes birth in whatever world (worldview) we have developed over time, begins showing (manifesting) beliefs about what our selves are composed of (i.e., the aggregates), and actively uses the senses to feed that sense of self ("obtaining the bases for contact"). We have become who we thought we should be, and we act like it.

In a sense, this "birth" closes the loop of *sankhara* by fulfilling that initial desire for creation. And where does this lead? See the next post.

NOTE: A more thorough explanation of the meaning of "birth" in dependent origination is to be found in my paper "Burning Yourself".

#12 Aging and Death

The final field of dependent arising is "aging and death"—a metonym[74] for impermanence and *dukkha*. On a literal level, if it were not for aging and death—for things being impermanent—there would be no *dukkha* at all. If we always were able to keep the things we obtained and found we enjoyed—if they were permanent—we would not ever suffer for the loss of the things we made a part of our lives. In this way, literal aging and death are the field in which the final result of the twelve links grows: our misery feeds on the impermanence represented by the way things age and pass away, and on the way **we** age and pass away, too. Every aspect of the world that we find necessary to our sense of who we are will change, will eventually be lost. Every definition we create in an attempt to make the world seem stable and knowable will also prove

[74] Thanks to Professor Gombrich for introducing me to a very useful word. It means the use of the name of one object or concept for another related object or concept, e.g. 'wheels' for 'car'.

impermanent because all things are unstable and not completely knowable.

> The aging of beings in the various orders of beings, their old age, brokenness of teeth, grayness of hair, wrinkling of skin, decline of life, weakness of faculties—this is called aging. The passing of beings out of the various orders of beings, their passing away, dissolution, disappearance, dying, completion of time, dissolution of the aggregates, laying down of the body—this is called death. So this aging and this death are what is called aging and death.—MN 9 translated by Bhikkhus Nanamoli and Bodhi

In other suttas this step is given greater range with "sorrow, lamentation, pain, grief and despair" [MN 11] and this is the actual point: that all the efforts we have put into our understanding of the way the world works, and the way we fit into it, and what we are supposed to do to make our lot better—all the times we argue with others about what it's all about and ignore their good points, and focus on their failures in logic, completely miss when someone pulls apart our logic, and only notice when we score a point—all that effort, all our certainty about how if we just get this one more possession, achieve this one more goal, do one more retreat, get one more raise, get one more lover we will finally be happy—all that ends, not in bliss, but in *dukkha*, in sorrow and lamentation. This is where all our efforts at putting the world together in a way that will make us happy, and protecting that self to an excessive degree, tend to lead: not towards safety and comfort, but towards false expectations and misplaced energy.

We're not going to end our aging or prevent our death with our practice—as much as the literal description might lead us to think that's what this step is about—what it's really asking us to do is to notice how making our sense of who we are dependent on things that aren't really part of us, things that (like us) won't last—leads to all that misery. This is not to say that we shouldn't enjoy things that are impermanent; it only says that we shouldn't make our happiness so contingent on them that when they pass away we feel like we died too. Recognizing the impermanence of whatever we love, and that it will pass away (or we will) lets us more fully appreciate what we have in the moments we have it.

#0: The Taints

> There are three taints: the taint of sensual desire, the taint of being and the taint of ignorance. With the arising of ignorance there is the arising of the taints. With the cessation of ignorance there is the cessation of the taints. The way leading to the cessation of the taints is just this Noble Eightfold Path; that is, right view, right intention, right speech, right action, right livelihood, right effort, right mindfulness and right concentration.—MN 9 Bhikkhus Nanamoli & Bodhi's translation.

The usual starting place for dependent origination is with ignorance, but way back at the beginning of these posts, in the sutta cited above, when Sariputta defined ignorance in the structure usually applied to the four noble truths (what is ignorance, what is its origin, its cessation, the path to its cessation?) he said that the arising of the taints brought the arising of ignorance, and the cessation of the taints ended ignorance, so we could say that dependent arising goes one more step back from ignorance—except that we can see from the above, that ignorance is one of the taints. How's that work?

First, if we look at the other two—sensual desire (kama) and being (bhava)—we might find that these have their source in ignorance, too: both can represent our natural tendency to follow one path or another around beliefs in the self: the belief that sensual desires will make us happy, or the belief that the becoming of the self will lead to ultimate bliss—both of these beliefs are founded on the ignorance we've just explored in depth through those twelve links—so what we seem to have here is ignorance, ignorance, and more ignorance.

On a more practical level—one we can see for ourselves if we just look around—it's quite true that ignorance breeds ignorance when it comes to *dukkha* and what's being described in dependent arising. Modern science, when it tells us about confirmation bias, tells us that we will protect our most cherished ideas from any threat by doing just what has been described by the Buddha here—by liking what is like us and our ideas, by rejecting what is not like us and our ideas—this is exactly our ignorance feeding more ignorance because it keeps us from seeing that others may know things we don't know, and our conclusions may be based on less information than we need or could have to make them.

In the final analysis, ignorance is the root of the problem, and knowledge is the cure, but it is a very specific ignorance, and very specific knowledge. As long as we are unaware of the way we come into the world with a need for a sense-of-self, a need that—in its excesses—gets us into trouble, we can't find a way out of the problem. The first links in the chain of causation describe the situation we are born into, a way of being that goes back as far as we can see—to the birth of "the First Man", or really, to our origins as described by our myths. What's pointed out is the way we are driven by this need for the self to exist, a need that drives us to seek confirmation of who we are and what part we play in the individuality of everything around us, information we seek through our senses. This drive gets detailed in a sequence—loosely modeled on Vedic rituals—that describes the rituals we (in our ignorance) perform of seeking confirmation of the self through our senses, interpreting it in ways that support our sense of who we are and the way the world works, and developing our interpretation into increasingly dogmatic views, until we bring to birth a sense of self that is visible to the world through our actions. But, because we are mistaken in so many of our assumptions (and we are blinded by our ignorance of the way things are working—at a very deep level—into being sure we are right in those assumptions) all our efforts lead not to the bliss we'd like, but to a tangle of problems so deeply interwoven into our lives that—without specific help to see what's going on—most of us won't be able to find a way out.

Dependent arising describes the problem, and in so doing, gives us the knowledge we need to effect a cure. It all comes down to ending those "taints"—the natural confusion about what's going on that has us wanting this or wanting that, thinking it will satisfy our cravings. As long as we don't recognize the deepest basis for our cravings, we can never break free. As soon as we realize that our sense that "This is good, I like this, it suits me, it fits with my worldview, it satisfies" is all about comforting ourselves about our selves, we are on the road to recovery.

The Words of Dependent Arising: *Sankhara*

Chapter 3: The Words of Dependent Arising: Sankhara

aka **"Everything you wanted to know about sankharas but were afraid to ask."**

Over on the blog at the Secular Buddhist Association website, I did a series on a secular approach to dependent arising, and in the comments for the second post, I was asked if I could give specific examples of *sankharas*, because the suttas we have—and the word choices used in the translations ("formations" "fabrications" "activities") or lack of them (some translations just skip the word altogether) make it very difficult to understand what is being said. I said I'd give it a try, but in a brief survey of the many mentions of *sankhara*, I found that there aren't "examples" as such, at least not in the way that one might have examples of something like *vedana* (feelings, experiences) which are described sometimes as pleasant, unpleasant, or neither. We are given stories that can be seen to illustrate feelings, like the one of the jealous guy who sees his woman talking to another man—the feelings that arise there are examples of *vedana*, and the thoughts that arise, and ideas for what to do about the situation afterward could be seen to express the *tanha* and *upadana* that follow.

But the *sankharas* don't get treated that way, probably because they aren't so much things that happen in our lives, rather, they are underlying tendencies or overall concepts that affect our lives. They get described in a variety of ways, some of which tell us what they look like when they become visible. They become visible as "the actions that are a result of their impact on us", so we could say that the action the jealous man takes is a *sankhara* because it is a *sankhara*-made-visible. But his jealousy is also a *sankhara*, too, it's a *sankhara*-keenly-felt.

Because *sankhara* is the second term in a conditional chain of events, really, every step afterward is a *sankhara* in that same sense: the consciousness that arises next is *sankhara*-consciousness, because *sankhara* drives it, and in just the same way, it drives every step thereafter.

In working on this, I came to see that what a *sankhara* is, is a drive. It has limitations on it, like ignorance does, as described in an earlier blogpost on my website[75]. When I say it is "a drive" I don't mean just any old drive. It is a very specific drive: a drive for the existence of and protection of and knowledge of the self, a very driven-drive, a slightly over-the-top drive on the best of days, and a very over-the-top drive on the worst of them.

It gets this meaning from the Prajapati myth that is embedded in the first five steps of dependent arising, where *sankhara* is the craving for existence that brings the universe into being. This leads me to believe that "drive" may be the best all-around translation of *sankhara*. We can also see the way in which the steps after *sankharas* are all *sankharas*, themselves: because every step drives the next.

To test this out, and since I'm not finding jealousy-level examples of *sankhara*-as-a-drive in the suttas, I figured the next best thing was to find suttas in which *sankharas* are discussed or described, and see if putting the word "drive" in there makes those sections easier to understand. As a starting point, I used Nanavira Thera's "Notes on Dhamma" to pull up explanations of, and references to, *sankharas*, and then wrote my own translation of those bits. I first did a translation that maintained grammatical correctness, and then rewrote it to be more easily read by a modern audience. I did not maintain traditional translations of other words in these pieces (because I feel, after looking at the word origins, that several of them miss the point as well).

I am hoping that gathering so many pieces on *sankhara* together in this one post will help in understanding the part it plays not just in dependent arising, but in the "aggregates" as well. See what you think.

I provide the Pali for my translations, followed by my translation of the passage using "drive" for "*sankhara*". For your reference, links are given in footnotes to sutta citations, to give you an idea of how the passage has been translated in the past.

SN 12.2 (pts S ii 4)[76]

> *katame ca, bhikkhave, saṅkhārā? tayome, bhikkhave, saṅkhārā—kāyasaṅhāro, vacīsaṅkhāro, cittasaṅkhāro. ime vuccanti, bhikkhave, saṅkhārā.*

---

[75] `http://justalittledust.com/blog/?p=1124`

[76] `http://nanavira.org/index.php?option=com_content&task=view&id=34&Itemid=62#p5` beginning with "And which, monks, are determinations?"

> And what kinds of drives are there? Drives are of three types: that which drives the body, that which drives speech, and that which drives thoughts."

That seems simple enough to me. Not a lot of detail there, but more is coming.

MN 44 (pts M i 301)[77]

> *"katamo panāyye, kāyasaṅkhāro, katamo vacīsaṅkhāro, katamo cittasaṅkhāro"ti?*
>
> *"assāsapassāsā kho, āvuso visākha, kāyasaṅkhāro, vitakkavicārā vacīsaṅkhāro, saññā ca vedanā ca cittasaṅkhāro"ti.*
>
> *"kasmā panāyye, assāsapassāsā kāyasaṅkhāro, kasmā vitakkavicārā vacīsaṅkhāro, kasmā saññā ca vedanā ca cittasaṅkhāro"ti?*
>
> *"assāsapassāsā kho, āvuso visākha, kāyikā ete dhammā kāyappaṭibaddhā, tasmā assāsapassāsā kāyasaṅkhāro. pubbe kho, āvuso visākha, vitakketvā vicāretvā pacchā vācaṃ bhindati, tasmā vitakkavicārā vacīsaṅkhāro. saññā ca vedanā ca cetasikā ete dhammā cittappaṭibaddhā, tasmā saññā ca vedanā ca cittasaṅkhāro"ti.*

> "But what is that which drives the body, that which drives speech, and that which drives thoughts?"
>
> "Breathing is a driver of the body. Thought and evaluation are drivers of speech. Perceptions and experience drive thoughts."
>
> "But why is breathing a driver of the body? Why are thought and evaluation drivers of speech? How do perceptions and experiences drive thoughts?"
>
> "Breathing is physical; the body certainly depends on it. That's why breathing is a driver of the body. Because we first think and evaluate before speaking, that's why thought and evaluation are drivers of speech. Perceptions and experiences happen in the mind; the mind depends on them. That's why perceptions and experiences drive thoughts."

This makes it clear why *sankhara* gets identified with breathing—it's not that when we stop *sankhara* as part of liberation, we need to stop breathing! It's just that breathing drives the body. In the Buddha's day, the breath was often thought of as the life-force, and it seems to be brought up here, in part, to address its importance. It may also

[77] `http://www.accesstoinsight.org/tipitaka/mn/mn.044.than.html#agg3` beginning with "But what are bodily fabrications?"

be touching on the way our breathing changes in response to various situations—when we can calm the breathing, it is no longer "driving" the body in the same way (this gets touched on in a later passage related to meditation).

The primary point in each of these, though, discusses the mundane requirements for each of the three (body, speech, mind). This is actually another way of discussing "nutriment" or the most foundational element that goes into the process. At the most obvious level, these are the foundations we would not want to have go away. We aren't wanting to give up breathing, or thinking and evaluating, or being able to perceive our experiences. We might, however, pay attention to each of these to see if we can use them to find the actual problems: a change in our breathing can act as an alarm telling us something new is going on; certain thoughts and evaluations may contribute to our problems; certain perceptions of experiences would, too.

In the translation below I have tried to capture *cetanā*'s meaning of thoughts that will become visible through action. It is usually translated as "intention" but in our culture "intention" has a conscious quality to it that I think is not appropriate here because the "thoughts" are actually "drives" and, as such, are below what we would call the conscious level. I'm also trying out "dhamma" as "things we are certain of"—the "truths" we rely on (which is a whole 'nuther article):

SN 22.56 (pts S iii 60)[78]

> *"katame ca, bhikkhave, saṅkhārā? chayime, bhikkhave, cetanākāyā—rūpasañcetanā, saddasañcetanā, gandhasañcetanā, rasasañcetanā, phoṭṭhabbasañcetanā, dhammasañcetanā. ime vuccanti, bhikkhave, saṅkhārā. phassasamudayā saṅkhārasamudayo; phassanirodhā saṅkhāranirodho."*

> "And what, monks, are drives? There are six types of thoughts that will drive actions: there are those thoughts driven by visual qualities, by sounds, by scents, by tastes, by tactile qualities, and by certainties (dhamma). These are called drives. With the rise of contact, there is the rise of the drives."

This makes it clear why, in some suttas, link #6, "contact" is suddenly found preceding link #2 "*sankhara*". This apparent "lack of order" has confused many people over the years. The reason is that the first five

[78] `http://www.accesstoinsight.org/tipitaka/sn/sn22/sn22.056.than.html #bods6` beginning "And what are fabrications?"

links are an overview describing how we come to act the way we do, and only with link #6 do we begin to get a description of that acting. It begins with contact through the senses that touches on and fires off that drive we've been told about. Contact makes the drive visible through what happens next.

In the passages above, the *sankharas* have been examined from the perspective of how they appear to us, and how they happen: they are made visible by our bodies, and our speech, and through our thoughts; they are set off by contact through the senses. Below, we consider the direction that these drives lead in, which gives us a different way of categorizing the *sankharas*, in terms of their results. This is the sense in which *sankharas* often get associated with karma, which is of a paralleling "three types".

SN 12.51 (pts S ii 82)[79]

> *"avijjāgato yaṃ, bhikkhave, purisapuggalo puññaṃ ce saṅkhāraṃ abhisaṅkharoti, puññūpagaṃ hoti viññāṇaṃ. apuññaṃ ce saṅkhāraṃ abhisaṅkharoti, apuññūpagaṃ hoti viññāṇaṃ. āneñjaṃ ce saṅkhāraṃ abhisaṅkharoti āneñjūpagaṃ hoti viññāṇaṃ. yato kho, bhikkhave, bhikkhuno avijjā pahīnā hoti vijjā uppannā, so avijjāvirāgā vijjuppādā neva puññābhisaṅkhāraṃ abhisaṅkharoti na apuññābhisaṅkhāraṃ abhisaṅkharoti na āneñjābhisaṅkhāraṃ abhisaṅkharoti. anabhisaṅkharonto anabhisañcetayanto na kiñci loke upādiyati; anupādiyaṃ na paritassati, aparitassaṃ paccattaññeva parinibbāyati. 'khīṇā jāti, vusitaṃ brahmacariyaṃ, kataṃ karaṇīyaṃ, nāparaṃ itthattāyā'ti pajānāti."*

> "Monks, if a person in a state of ignorance is engaged with a beneficial drive, their awareness seeks the beneficial; if engaged with a harmful drive, their awareness seeks the harmful; if engaged with a static drive, their awareness moves on to the stable. But when a person has left behind ignorance and has come to deep wisdom, there is no engagement with beneficial drives, or harmful drives, or static drives. Then, unengaged with drives, there is no more being caught up in the world. Not caught, there is no more disturbance. Undisturbed, that person attains complete calm, and the understanding that 'Birth is finished, the highest conduct has been achieved, what needed to be done has been done, there is no other state following this.'"

Notice that there is mention of being totally unengaged with *sankhara* of any kind—not the beneficial, not the harmful, not the neutral

[79] No online reference to cite.

sort. Examining this passage tells us that the end of *sankhara* is simply about not being caught up in the world anymore—not being driven by ignorance-contact—with no more problematic states of mind following on. Nothing is said about lack of will to live. This is because the drives being discussed aren't the useful drives that give us the basics that we need to survive, they are the excessive drives—they are the natural drive for survival taken a bit too far.

The passage below is not included in Nanavira's consideration of *sankhara*, but it follows on so nicely from the one above, that it seemed to me I should include it. It also may help to explain why "breath" is the driver for bodily *sankharas*.

SN 36.11 (pts S iv 216)[80]

> *"...tisso imā, bhikkhu, vedanā vuttā mayā. sukhā vedanā, dukkhā vedanā, adukkhamasukhā vedanā—imā tisso vedanā vuttā mayā. vuttaṃ kho panetaṃ, bhikkhu, mayā—'yaṃ kiñci vedayitaṃ, taṃ dukkhasmin'ti. taṃ kho panetaṃ, bhikkhu, mayā saṅkhārānaṃyeva aniccataṃ sandhāya bhāsitaṃ—'yaṃ kiñci vedayitaṃ taṃ dukkhasmin'ti. taṃ kho panetaṃ, bhikkhu, mayā saṅkhārānaṃyeva khayadhammataṃ...pe...vayadhammataṃ...pe...virāgadhammataṃ...pe...nirodhadhammataṃ...pe...vipariṇāmadhammataṃ sandhāya bhāsitaṃ—'yaṃ kiñci vedayitaṃ taṃ dukkhasmin'ti. atha kho pana, bhikkhu, mayā anupubbasaṅkhārānaṃ nirodho akkhāto. paṭhamaṃ jhānaṃ samāpannassa vācā niruddhā hoti. dutiyaṃ jhānaṃ samāpannassa vitakkavicārā niruddhā honti. tatiyaṃ jhānaṃ samāpannassa pīti niruddhā hoti. catutthaṃ jhānaṃ samāpannassa assāsapassāsā niruddhā honti.*
>
> (The Buddha speaking): "Monks, I have mentioned these three experiences (*vedanā*): of the pleasant, unpleasant, and neither pleasant nor unpleasant... I have also said "Whatever is experienced, falls within the unpleasant." Regarding this, I have said this in reference only to drives' impermanence: "Whatever is experienced, falls within the unpleasant." Moreover, I have said this with reference only to the destruction of states of certainty that are the result of drives ... the loss of states of certainty that are the result of drives ... the indifference towards states of certainty ... the cessation of states of certainty ... the reversal of states of certainty that are the result of drives. "Whatever is experienced, falls within the unpleasant."

80 `http://www.accesstoinsight.org/tipitaka/sn/sn36/sn36.011.than.html` from "These three feelings have been spoken of by me"

> "I have also declared the drives' gradual cessation. On entering the first jhana, speech vanishes. On entering the second jhana, reflection and deliberation vanish. On entering the third jhana, delight vanishes. On entering the fourth jhana, in-and-out breathing vanishes... ."

In the first paragraph above, it seems clear to me that the Buddha is saying that when he talks about experience (aka "feeling") always being unpleasant (*dukkhasmin*)—despite the way he elsewhere describes it as pleasant, unpleasant, or neutral—he is specifically talking about it in reference to experience that takes part in dependent arising—experience that is driven by the *sankhara*-drives. When we are contacted through our senses, if there is a drive toward (for example) beneficial acts, the pleasant/unpleasant/neutral experience that results is always bound up with *dukkha*; it may feel "pleasant" but it is still going to result in *dukkha*, because it is driven by the need for an (over-the-top) sense of self. It is not that the pleasant is actually unpleasant (it is not that all experience can be immediately felt as *dukkha*, or should be), it is that even pleasant experiences—the ones that are grounded in ignorance and driven by the *sankhara*-drives—lead to *dukkha* ("the unpleasant").

In the second paragraph, the four jhanas are related to the three visible forms the *sankharas* take. Speech goes away first, as one sits silently; thought fades with the second; the third picks up the extra slot, having that sensation of joy and rapture that can be a part of meditation fade away; the fourth is usually translated as the cessation of breath, but all four make just as much sense (and the Pali justifies) all four of them "vanishing"—at least to the perspective of the meditator's awareness.

And then we have the classic triad:

KN 2.20 Dhammapada 277-279[81]

> *sabbe saṅkhārā aniccā... sabbe saṅkhārā dukkhā... sabbe dhammā anattā*
>
> All drives are impermanent... All drives are *dukkha*... All certainties are not self.

I think the above speaks for itself.

Below we have *sankhara* as one of the five aggregates that get mistaken for self. "I am my drive to survive" seems like a logical belief for

[81] `http://www.accesstoinsight.org/tipitaka/kn/dhp/dhp.20.than.html` from "All fabrications are inconstant"

the uninstructed to have, to me.

MN 35 (pts M i 228)[82]

> *"rūpaṃ, bhikkhave, aniccaṃ, vedanā aniccā, saññā aniccā, saṅkhārā aniccā, viññāṇaṃ aniccaṃ. rūpaṃ, bhikkhave, anattā, vedanā anattā, saññā anattā, saṅkhārā anattā, viññāṇaṃ anattā. sabbe saṅkhārā aniccā, sabbe dhammā anattā"ti.*
>
> "Form, monks, is impermanent. Experience, perception, drives, and awareness are impermanent. Form is not-self, experience is not-self, perception, drives, and awareness are not-self. All drives are impermanent, all certainties are not-self."

Next up, as if seeing *sankharas* three ways—in terms of what makes them arise (contact with the senses), and what makes them visible (actions in body, speech, thought), and where they lead (to benefit, harm, or neither)—isn't enough, here's one more way to look at them: they drive the way we see ourselves, as the five aggregates. If we perceive of self as form, then when we come into contact with the world, we will perceive self as form; if we perceive self as our experience, then *sankhara* will drive us to bring about a sense-of-self as experience; if we perceive of ourselves as "the perceiver" we will get confirmation that's how it is and thereby bring about an active sense of self as "the perceiver"; if we think of ourselves as being our drives, we'll find that's what we are; same for awareness. We can see this as "they drive how we see ourselves" or "they drive the appearance of what we mistake for the self as it becomes visible in the world" (which would bring us back to action, both in terms of body, speech, and thought, and actions that are beneficial, harmful, or neither).

SN 22.79 (pts S iii 87)[83]

> *"kiñca, bhikkhave, saṅkhāre vadetha? saṅkhatamabhisaṅkharontīti kho, bhikkhave, tasmā 'saṅkhārā'ti vuccati. kiñca saṅkhatamabhisaṅkharonti? rūpaṃ rūpattāya saṅkhatamabhisaṅkharonti, vedanaṃ vedanattāya saṅkhatamabhisaṅkharonti, saññaṃ saññattāya saṅkhatamabhisaṅkharonti, saṅkhāre saṅkhārattāya saṅkhatamabhisaṅkharonti, viññāṇaṃ viññāṇattāya saṅkhatamabhisaṅkharonti. saṅkhatamabhisaṅkharontīti kho, bhikkhave, tasmā 'saṅkhārā'ti vuccati.*

82 `http://www.accesstoinsight.org/tipitaka/mn/mn.035.than.html` starting with "Form is inconstant. Feeling is inconstant."

83 `http://www.accesstoinsight.org/tipitaka/sn/sn22/sn22.079.than.html` from "And why do you call them 'fabrications'?"

> "And why do you call them 'drives'? Because they drive the driven, therefore they are called 'drives'. What is driven by the drive? In order to bring about form, drives drive form. In order to bring about experience, drives drive experience. In order to bring about perception, drives drive perception. In order to bring about drives, drives drive drives. In order to bring about awareness, drives drive awareness. Because they drive the driven, therefore they are called 'drives'."

To put it another way, we shouldn't be reading this as "*sankhara* creates form", but as "*sankhara* gets us to perceive self-as-form". *Sankhara* is all about drives that create our sense of self, not our actual physical selves.

Below is one last sutta I found that I think indicates the social aspects of *sankhara*—that the whole problem does not lie in us, and our perceptions of the world, but that we are often inspired by others' ways of thinking and being, and we follow them. It's not very explicit, so I'm not sure that I have the best understanding of it (I will keep an eye out for any other indications that the Buddha saw *sankhara* as being able to be a "joint venture" and hope you will point out to me any you find, too). It also points out that we get in trouble through *sankhara*'s influence whether it is when we are making conscious choices, or just acting without forethought.

SN 12.25 (pts S ii 40)[84]

> *sāmaṃ vā taṃ, ānanda, manosaṅkhāraṃ abhisaṅkharoti yaṃpaccayāssa taṃ uppajjati ajjhattaṃ sukhadukkhaṃ. pare vā taṃ, ānanda, manosaṅkhāraṃ abhisaṅkharonti yaṃpaccayāssa taṃ uppajjati ajjhattaṃ sukhadukkhaṃ. sampajāno vā taṃ, ānanda . . . pe . . . asampajāno vā taṃ, ānanda, manosaṅkhāraṃ abhisaṅkharoti yaṃpaccayāssa taṃ uppajjati ajjhattaṃ sukhadukkhaṃ.*
>
> Either driven by oneself, or because of another person, inward pleasure and pain arise, driven into existence by that which drives the mind. Either through forethought, or through lack of forethought, inward pleasure and pain arise, driven into existence by that which drives the mind.

Finally, there is a variation on the term we need to consider briefly. It's *āyusaṅkhārā* where *āyu* means "age" or "vitality" and gets extended to mean "life force", so that when it gets combined with *sankhara*, it

[84] `http://www.accesstoinsight.org/tipitaka/sn/sn12/sn12.025.than.html` after "From ignorance as a requisite condition, then"

can be seen to mean, literally, the drive that keeps us alive, that keeps us aging. It gets used in MN 43 (pts M i 296) in the answer to a question about whether or not that drive-for-living is *vedana* (a feeling or experience) or not—and Sariputta says it is not, or with the cessation of feeling in *jhana*, the meditator would never return! This is because, if "the drive to stay alive" were one of dependent arising's categories of feelings/experiences, then when one went into meditative states that brought an end to those problematic experiences, one would lose the will to live, and therefore die. (I note however, that—as in the sutta described below—the Buddha is said to have lost his drive to stay alive three months before he actually did die.) That *āyusaṅkhārā* is described as not being *vedana* does not mean we can't feel or experience that desire to keep living, either—it just means that when we feel it we are feeling something that is not included within dependent origination.

In the sutta that talks about *āyusaṅkhārā* there is also an interesting follow-up discussion immediately afterward, about the difference between being dead, and one who reaches the higher states of meditation. In that section the word *āyu* ("vitality") gets separated from *sankhara*, but *sankhara* comes up again in reference to bodily- verbal- and mental-*sankharas*—it's worth reading to see that "the will to live" would not be part of what goes away when liberated. This is also demonstrated in DN 16 (pts D ii 107) where, three months prior to his death, the Buddha gave up his *āyusaṅkhārā*—which means he had had that positive, reasonable drive all along, because it is not one of the the *sankharas* grounded in ignorance of *dukkha*.

To end the post, I'd like to include the *sankhara* reference I am currently most fond of, in which Mara questions the nun Vajira about the origins of beings, and she comes back with a pointed answer:

SN 5.10 (pts S i 135)[85]

> *"kiṃ nu sattoti paccesi, māra diṭṭhigataṃ nu te.*
> *suddhasaṅkhārapuñjoyaṃ, nayidha sattupalabbhati.*
>
> What's this?
> Do you believe in "a being", Mara?
> Have you arrived at a view?
> This is simply a mass of drives.
> Here in this world no being exists.

85 `http://www.accesstoinsight.org/tipitaka/sn/sn05/sn05.010.bodh.html` from "Why now do you assume?"

Appendix & Index

Appendix

Bibliography of Resources (mentioned in this book, and otherwise recommended)

Books

Bodhi, Bhikkhu
Connected Discourses of the Buddha: A Translation of the Saṃyutta Nikāya (2000) ISBN 0-86171-331-1
Numerical Discourses of the Buddha: A Translation of the Aṅguttara Nikāya (2012) ISBN 978-1-61429-040-7

Bodhi, Bhikkhu and Nanamoli Thera
Middle Length Discourses of the Buddha: A Translation of the Majjhima Nikāya (1995) ISBN 0-86171-072-X

Dawkins, Richard
The Selfish Gene (1976) ISBN 978-0192860927

DeGraff, Geoffrey aka Thanissaro Bhikkhu
Handful Of Leaves Series in print edition, but otherwise available online (see Websites: accesstoinsight.org)

Gombrich, Richard
How Buddhism Began (1996) ISBN 0-415-37123-6
What The Buddha Thought (2009) ISBN 978-1-84553-614-5

Jurewicz, Joanna
Fire and Cognition in the Rgveda (2010) ISBN 978-83-7151-893-5

Nanavira Thera
Clearing the Path (1963, 1987, 2010) ISBN 978-94-6090-004-4
Notes on Dhamma (1963, 1987, 2009) ISBN 978-90-6090-001-3

Olivelle, Patrick
Upaniṡads (1996) ISBN 978-0-19-283576-5

Walshe, Maurice
Long Discourses of the Buddha: A Translation of the Dīgha Nikāya (1987, 1995) ISBN 0-86171-103-3

Journals

Journal of the Oxford Buddhist Centre for Buddhist Studies
`http://www.ocbs.org/journal`

Journal of the Pali Text Society
`http://www.palitext.com/palitext/jours.htm`

Articles

Jurewicz, Joanna, "Playing With Fire"
Journal of the Pali Text Society, Vol. XXVI (2000)

Websites

accesstoinsight.org
A great source for translations of the Pali canon.
dhammawheel.com
A large, well-moderated forum from a primarily Theravadan perspective full of open-minded contributors, many of whom have an excellent grasp of Buddhism and the texts.
justalittledust.com/blog/
My own blog, irregularly attended to.
nanavira.org
The writings of Ñāṇavīra Thera are freely available on this site. Dense going unless you're willing to take on the Pali but well worth doing.
secularbuddhism.com (Secular Buddhist Association website)
A collaborative work-in-progress designed to develop the conversation about how Buddhism can be applied for those who prefer a naturalistic approach to practice. In addition to the blog and discussion forum, the free podcast (available at the site as well as through iTunes) is one of many marvelous resources gathered here.
meaningness.wordpress.com
David Chapman's exploration of Buddhism past, present, and future.

On Dependent Arising:

The following are some resources for reading other views of dependent arising. Internet URLs change with fair frequency; if these links do not work, you can use your favorite search engine to locate the texts, if they are still available online, by looking for the author's name and the title of the work.

Buddhadasa Bhikkhu: Paticcasamuppada: Practical Dependent Origination
Buddhadhasa Bhikkhu was a Theravadan monastic.
`http://www.what-buddha-taught.net/Books6/Bhikkhu_Buddhadasa_Paticcasamuppada.htm`

Lama Zopa Rinpoche: The Twelve Links of Dependent Origination
The Rinpoche is of the Tibetan lineage.
`http://www.bodhicitta.net/Wheel of Life.htm`

MacPhillamy, Rev. Master Daizu: Dependent Origination Through A Microscope
Coming from the Zen lineage.
`http://www.pinemtnbuddhisttemple.org/dharma_articles/Dependent Origination Through a Microscope, RM Daizui.pdf`

Ñāṇavīra Thera: Notes on Dhamma: A Note on *Paṭicca Samuppāda*
Ñāṇavīra Thera was a Theravadan monk, and Englishman, who lived and died in Sri Lanka.
`http://nanavira.org/index.php?option=com_content&task=view&id=34&Itemid=62`

Thanissaro Bhikkhu: The Shape of Suffering
Thanissaro Bhikkhu is a Theravadan translator.
`http://www.accesstoinsight.org/lib/authors/thanissaro/shapeofsuffering.pdf`

Thrangu Rinpoche: The Twelve Links of Interdependent Origination
The Rinpoche is of the Tibetan lineage.
`http://www.rinpoche.com/teachings/12links.pdf`

And on the extended, liberative version of dependent arising:

Bodhi, Bhikkhu: Transcendental Dependent Arising
Bhikkhu Bodhi is a Theravadan translator.
`http://www.accesstoinsight.org/lib/authors/bodhi/wheel277.html`

On Pali:

Warder, A.K., Introduction to Pali (1963, 1974, 2005)
ISBN 0-86013-197-1. A classic textbook you can use to teach yourself Pali.

Digital Pali Reader
Makes delving into the Pali so easy it's almost nibbana. All the suttas online in Pali, with links to English translations where available. Click on a word in Pali and it'll give you its best guess how to parse it, and offer dictionary entries. Constantly being improved, but it's already a world-class tool.
`http://sourceforge.net/projects/digitalpali/`

Pali Lookup
Handy desktop application.
`http://pali-lookup.software.informer.com/`

A Note On The Index

Note: The index begins with Pali and Sanskrit terms (in English alphabetical order) and then goes on to English terms in their normal order (though proper names that include accents might appear to be 'out of order' – see for example 'Sāriputta'). Some Pali or Sanskrit terms are already a part of the English language so, even when they appear in their original language in the text (as does 'karma' in the paper 'Burning Yourself') they appear in the plain English section of the index. I have also put 'dukkha' and 'sankhara' in the English section because I would like them to be treated as the preferred term, which might have them, eventually, become accepted—unaccented—in English.

Index

About The Author

I have no credentialed authority on anything at all[86]; I am not a former Buddhist monk, nor a degreed scholar. I just have an ordinary person's working mind, and a background that favors critical thinking. There is nothing special about me that made it possible for me to see something 'impossible' for anyone to see before me; the reason I could see it is because it's not actually all that hard to see—it wasn't impossible to see, not in this day and age. It probably has been impossible until recently, though: a structure buried under centuries of dust, its pattern dimly seen, and guessed at, affecting all the pieces that bump up against it, but lost like the entrance to King Tut's tomb, until the winds of scholarship shifted the sands enough so that this amateur explorer stepped on a soft spot and fell right into a wonder. If it hadn't been me who saw it, someone else would have eventually.

I recognize that the hypothesis contained in this book makes for a revolutionary view of what the Buddha taught, and that many will be reluctant to even entertain the possibility that I might have spotted something others have missed, much less embrace the concepts. But it might well be that one contributing factor to my seeing things that others haven't seen is actually because I have not been indoctrinated by monastic practice, or through directed studies. This would help explain why Prof. Jurewicz recognized the pattern first, since, although she is clearly a well-educated scholar, her specialty is not Buddhism, so though she knows enough about it to be able to have spotted how her specialty might apply, she was not locked in to preconceived notions about what she should be seeing in dependent arising.

But what's important is not who first noticed a pattern, what's important is the ideas themselves, especially their usefulness to others.

I very much like David Chapman's approach to this, on his (wonderful) web pages in which he is working out how tantra can be useful in our times. He says:

> This approach is quite possibly wrong. If so, it's probably better that it be advocated by a nobody, like me.
>
> The suggestions I have are pretty obvious. They're natural outgrowths from traditional and '70s-80s tantra, plus contemporary Western ideas. If I don't propose them, someone with credentials might. If the approach had a credentialed backer, perhaps some students would be misled by author-

[86] Except telephone repair.

> ity. Perhaps, too, if an authority advocated this approach, critics would be too polite to dispute it.[87]

What I am pointing out is not in the same class—this is an outgrowth of study of the Buddha's historic time, and an effort to get closer to the original concepts, not a newly evolved approach—but the point behind having a nobody introduce a different way of looking at things is a good one. If I'm mistaken in what I see, no one is going to hesitate to point it out.

I am actually hoping others will come along and do something more than simply say that they disagree with this approach—I am already aware that the existing texts can and are read a different way from the reading I am giving them (that this happens is consistent with my understanding of how the texts came to be as they are), so the fact that people see it differently is not news to me—but if others can show why this cannot be a correct interpretation, given the texts we have and their history, that would be very helpful. Others may be able to contribute positively to this work, as well; I feel sure that seeing dependent arising in this way will illuminate much of what is said in the suttas that has been confusing or just too fuzzy for us to really understand in the past, and those who pick up reading the Pali canon with this in mind may draw out deeper meanings that will help us all.

In the end, the ideas themselves will prove out or not. Philologists and philosphers can study the texts and see for themselves if the structure I'm pointing out is consistent with what's in the suttas or not. Sanskrit scholars may be able to point out whether the connections I've made seem valid or not, and perhaps find new ones. Buddhist practitioners can test out the insights I say are original to the Buddha to see if they strengthen the reduction of dukkha in their own lives or not—and if they do, that is surely to the Buddha's credit, not to mine. I am not the authority or the originator here, which is why who I am hardly matters.

About This Book

Dependent Arising In Context was typeset using the freely available (but quite challenging) LaTeX system (MiKTex 2.9, for Windows). The font used throughout the book is Bitstream Charter as distributed with

87 I highly recommend reading the whole of this blog, from start to finish. The quoted piece is taken from `http://meaningness.wordpress.com/2012/04/27/now-you-something-say/` but the entire work is both very well-written, and has useful and interesting points to make.

LaTeX. The cover fonts are Goudy Trajan Regular from CastleType, and Goudy Bookletter 1911 by Barry Schwartz. I am grateful to the designers for releasing these for commercial use.

Since the book was typeset by the author, and there is likely to be a "second edition" made from the same masters, if you notice typographical errors, spelling errors, or omissions, I would be grateful if you'd notify me, preferably by quoting the sentence the error is found in, and pointing out exactly what the problem is. This will improve the experience of the book for future readers. You can reach me via email at authorauthor@justalittledust.com for at least the next few years.

25467972R00082

Made in the USA
Middletown, DE
30 October 2015